W9-BKA-459

1895
main line
7-14-94

WITHDRAWN

DIZZY GILLESPIE

DIZZY GILLESPIE

❧

Tony Gentry

Senior Consulting Editor
Nathan Irvin Huggins
Director
W.E.B. Du Bois Institute for Afro-American Research
Harvard University

CHELSEA HOUSE PUBLISHERS
New York   Philadelphia

BALDWIN PUBLIC LIBRARY

Chelsea House Publishers
Editor-in-Chief   Remmel Nunn
Managing Editor   Karyn Gullen Browne
Copy Editor   Juliann Barbato
Picture Editor   Adrian G. Allen
Art Director   Maria Epes
Deputy Copy Chief   Mark Rifkin
Assistant Art Director   Noreen Romano
Manufacturing Manager   Gerald Levine
Systems Manager   Lindsey Ottman
Production Manager   Joseph Romano
Production Coordinator   Marie Claire Cebrián

Black Americans of Achievement

Senior Editor   Richard Rennert

Staff for **DIZZY GILLESPIE**

Editorial Assistant   Michele Haddad
Picture Researcher   Alan Gottlieb
Designer   Ghila Krajzman
Cover Illustration   Alan Nahigian

Copyright © 1991 by Chelsea House Publishers, a division of Main
Line Book Co. All rights reserved. Printed and bound in the United
States of America.

3   5   7   9   8   6   4

Library of Congress Cataloging-in-Publication Data

Gentry, Tony.
    Dizzy Gillespie: musician/by Tony Gentry.
      p.   cm.—(Black Americans of achievement)
    Includes bibliographical references and index.
    Summary: A biography of the Afro-American musician and
"ambassador of jazz" who introduced the world to bebop.
    ISBN 0-7910-1127-5
        0-7910-1152-6 (pbk.)
      1. Gillespie, Dizzy, 1917–   —Juvenile literature. 2. Jazz
musicians—United States—Biography—Juvenile literature.
[1. Gillespie, Dizzy, 1917–   . 2. Musicians. 3. Afro-
Americans—Biography.] I. Title. II. Series.
ML3930.G47G4 1991   90-23185
788.9'2165'092—dc20   CIP
[B]   AC MN

CONTENTS

BLACK AMERICANS OF ACHIEVEMENT

RALPH ABERNATHY
civil rights leader

MUHAMMAD ALI
heavyweight champion

RICHARD ALLEN
religious leader and social activist

LOUIS ARMSTRONG
musician

ARTHUR ASHE
tennis great

JOSEPHINE BAKER
entertainer

JAMES BALDWIN
author

BENJAMIN BANNEKER
scientist and mathematician

AMIRI BARAKA
poet and playwright

COUNT BASIE
bandleader and composer

ROMARE BEARDEN
artist

JAMES BECKWOURTH
frontiersman

MARY MCLEOD
BETHUNE
educator

BLANCHE BRUCE
politician

RALPH BUNCHE
diplomat

GEORGE WASHINGTON
CARVER
botanist

CHARLES CHESNUTT
author

BILL COSBY
entertainer

PAUL CUFFE
merchant and abolitionist

FATHER DIVINE
religious leader

FREDERICK DOUGLASS
abolitionist editor

CHARLES DREW
physician

W.E.B. DU BOIS
scholar and activist

PAUL LAURENCE DUNBAR
poet

KATHERINE DUNHAM
dancer and choreographer

MARIAN WRIGHT EDELMAN
civil rights leader and lawyer

DUKE ELLINGTON
bandleader and composer

RALPH ELLISON
author

JULIUS ERVING
basketball great

JAMES FARMER
civil rights leader

ELLA FITZGERALD
singer

MARCUS GARVEY
black-nationalist leader

DIZZY GILLESPIE
musician

PRINCE HALL
social reformer

W. C. HANDY
father of the blues

WILLIAM HASTIE
educator and politician

MATTHEW HENSON
explorer

CHESTER HIMES
author

BILLIE HOLIDAY
singer

JOHN HOPE
educator

LENA HORNE
entertainer

LANGSTON HUGHES
poet

ZORA NEALE HURSTON
author

JESSE JACKSON
civil rights leader and politician

JACK JOHNSON
heavyweight champion

JAMES WELDON JOHNSON
author

SCOTT JOPLIN
composer

BARBARA JORDAN
politician

MARTIN LUTHER KING, JR.
civil rights leader

ALAIN LOCKE
scholar and educator

JOE LOUIS
heavyweight champion

RONALD MCNAIR
astronaut

MALCOLM X
militant black leader

THURGOOD MARSHALL
Supreme Court justice

ELIJAH MUHAMMAD
religious leader

JESSE OWENS
champion athlete

CHARLIE PARKER
musician

GORDON PARKS
photographer

SIDNEY POITIER
actor

ADAM CLAYTON POWELL, JR.
political leader

LEONTYNE PRICE
opera singer

A. PHILIP RANDOLPH
labor leader

PAUL ROBESON
singer and actor

JACKIE ROBINSON
baseball great

BILL RUSSELL
basketball great

JOHN RUSSWURM
publisher

SOJOURNER TRUTH
antislavery activist

HARRIET TUBMAN
antislavery activist

NAT TURNER
slave revolt leader

DENMARK VESEY
slave revolt leader

MADAM C. J. WALKER
entrepreneur

BOOKER T. WASHINGTON
educator

HAROLD WASHINGTON
politician

WALTER WHITE
civil rights leader and author

RICHARD WRIGHT
author

ON ACHIEVEMENT

Coretta Scott King

BEFORE YOU BEGIN this book, I hope you will ask yourself what the word excellence means to you. I think that it's a question we should all ask, and keep asking as we grow older and change. Because the truest answer to it should never change. When you think of excellence, perhaps you think of success at work; or of becoming wealthy; or meeting the right person, getting married, and having a good family life.

Those important goals are worth striving for, but there is a better way to look at excellence. As Martin Luther King, Jr., said in one of his last sermons, "I want you to be first in love. I want you to be first in moral excellence. I want you to be first in generosity. If you want to be important, wonderful. If you want to be great, wonderful. But recognize that he who is greatest among you shall be your servant."

My husband, Martin Luther King, Jr., knew that the true meaning of achievement is service. When I met him, in 1952, he was already ordained as a Baptist preacher and was working towards a doctoral degree at Boston University. I was studying at the New England Conservatory and dreamed of accomplishments in music. We married a year later, and after I graduated the following year we moved to Montgomery, Alabama. We didn't know it then, but our notions of achievement were about to undergo a dramatic change.

You may have read or heard about what happened next. What began with the boycott of a local bus line grew into a national movement, and by the time he was assassinated in 1968 my husband had fashioned a black movement powerful enough to shatter forever the practice of racial segregation. What you may not have read about is where he got his method for resisting injustice without compromising his religious beliefs.

He adopted the strategy of nonviolence from a man of a different race, who lived in a distant country, and even practiced a different religion. The man was Mahatma Gandhi, the great leader of India, who devoted his life to serving humanity in the spirit of love and nonviolence. It was in these principles that Martin discovered his method for social reform. More than anything else, those two principles were the key to his achievements.

This book is about black Americans who served society through the excellence of their achievements. It forms a part of the rich history of black men and women in America—a history of stunning accomplishments in every field of human endeavor, from literature and art to science, industry, education, diplomacy, athletics, jurisprudence, even polar exploration.

Not all of the people in this history had the same ideals, but I think you will find something that all of them have in common. Like Martin Luther King, Jr., they all decided to become "drum majors" and serve humanity. In that principle—whether it was expressed in books, inventions, or song—they found something outside themselves to use as a goal and a guide. Something that showed them a way to serve others, instead of living only for themselves.

Reading the stories of these courageous men and women not only helps us discover the principles that we will use to guide our own lives but also teaches us about our black heritage and about America itself. It is crucial for us to know the heroes and heroines of our history and to realize that the price we paid in our struggle for equality in America was dear. But we must also understand that we have gotten as far as we have partly because America's democratic system and ideals made it possible.

We are still struggling with racism and prejudice. But the great men and women in this series are a tribute to the spirit of our democratic ideals and the system in which they have flourished. And that makes their stories special and worth knowing. ❧

DIZZY GILLESPIE

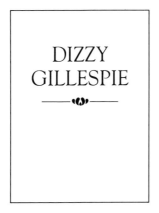

1

DIZZY SWINGS

———— ❦ ————

Trumpet virtuoso John Birks ("Dizzy") Gillespie at age 22, when he was struggling to develop the unique form of jazz that became known as bebop. "I wasn't the type to worry," he said, "as long as I could get enough food to have enough energy to play my horn. I just went on and played with all these bands, made all the sessions, until my chance came."

LISTEN TO THAT dizzy cat," trumpet player "Fats" Palmer Davis told himself as he slipped into the shadowy Philadelphia rehearsal hall one winter day in 1935. Alone on the bandstand sat the newest member of the Frankie Fairfax Band, an 18-year-old trumpet player named John Birks Gillespie. The teenager had laid down his trumpet, however, and was now testing his solos on the keyboard. Davis had rarely witnessed such a sight, a horn man who not only showed up early to practice but who could also play the piano.

But this kid was full of surprises. Always joking, dancing, mugging at the girls, he never seemed to sit still. And when he was on the bandstand, he put all that youthful energy into his music. Every night at the show, Gillespie tried to play each trumpet solo faster and with more notes than the one before. He was like a baseball slugger swinging for the fences. More often than not, he struck out, missing the impossibly high notes he tried to hit. But the next time his solo came around, he was swinging again, aiming to belt one out of the park. Davis gave him credit for trying. And he sounded good on the piano, too.

Gillespie stayed at the keyboard while the other band members filed in. Some thought he was just doodling, but others noticed how he seemed to take a melody apart and put it back together in unusual keys and at odd tempos. When Davis patted Gillespie's empty chair in the trumpet section and asked, "Hey, where's Dizzy?" they all laughed.

"Yeah, man," somebody added, "that's a good name for that cat, 'Dizzy.' Dizzy Gillespie."

Smiling broadly, the new kid jumped up from the piano bench. He could live with that. Any jazzman worth his salt had a nickname, and now he had one, too.

The Frankie Fairfax Band played swing music, fiercely rhythmic renditions of popular songs that brought audiences to their feet, spinning and tossing their partners to the fastest, wildest dance anybody had ever seen, the Lindy Hop. The whole country might be bogged down in the economic troubles of the Great Depression, but on the dance floor, prodded by the unrelenting drive of a hot swing band, young people knew they could forget their worries for a while.

Swing was far and away the most popular style of music in America during the mid-1930s, and to play in a big band had become one of the most cherished dreams of young musicians across the country. Gillespie felt proud to have landed a job with the Frankie Fairfax Band. He had fallen in love with the sharp clothes, racy slang, and easy confidence of the band members. Nothing could compare with the charge he got about halfway through a show, when the band had warmed up and the music swung with a locomotive's relentless power.

But the jazz world was not all fun and games. For a restless teenager, it could get boring playing the same songs every night. Gillespie tried to squeeze new rhythms, new tempos, a million screaming

notes, from low to high, into his solos, even though he knew that one trumpet player could never kick a band into high gear by himself. Nothing could keep him from trying, though.

Eventually, Gillespie began to itch for a change of scenery. A year after he was hired by Frankie Fairfax, the band's other two trumpeters, Charlie Shavers and Carl ("Bama") Warwick, joined a fancier outfit, the Lucky Millinder Band, in New York City. Gillespie asked his friends if they could get him a tryout with their new employer.

The day the two horn players called to say everything had been arranged, Gillespie ran home, kissed his mother good-bye, and jumped on the first train to New York. One of his older brothers, J.P., lived in a small walk-up apartment in the uptown district of Harlem. Dizzy moved in with him and waited to be hired by Lucky Millinder.

Gillespie (front row, second from right) with the Frankie Fairfax Band, the first jazz orchestra he ever joined. He received the nickname Dizzy shortly after he landed a spot with the group in 1935.

In the meantime, the teenager toured the busy city he had heard about all his life. All the people on the streets, all the traffic, restaurants, and music clubs, suited him perfectly. New York moved fast, but if you paid attention, the jutting buildings, blaring horns, jackhammers, subway trains, and bright lights blended with the fragrant aromas from barbecued-rib joints and peanut stands into a thrilling sensation that was almost musical.

For days, Gillespie strolled the streets, enjoying all of it. Sometimes he blew chewing-gum bubbles to exercise his lungs, the satisfying pink pop punctuating the riotous sounds around him. He had actually made it to New York City, where the jazz masters lived, to join a big band! He could hardly believe his good fortune.

For a while, Lucky Millinder kept Gillespie on salary; but Dizzy, as it turned out, was never offered a permanent job. The young trumpet player sounded too rough edged and undisciplined for the smooth style of music that Millinder favored. Dejected, Gillespie packed up his horn and went back to his brother's apartment to figure out what to do next.

Fingering the trumpet valves as he stared out the window, Gillespie realized he had three choices. He could go home to his mother in Philadelphia and try to rejoin the Frankie Fairfax Band; but after a few weeks in New York, Philadelphia seemed like a quiet backwater. He could look for a day job washing dishes—lots of musicians paid the rent that way— and make the rounds of the jazz clubs after dark; but then when would he find the time to practice his trumpet? Or he could put all his eggs in one basket and swear to live or die by his horn.

While Gillespie pondered his options, the sounds of crying babies, radio music, sizzling fry pans, and ribald laughter drifted into the apartment from an air shaft near the window. The air shaft acted like a megaphone, amplifying all the sounds of the neigh-borhood, and there was a sort of rhythm to these sounds that seemed to exist just beyond the reach of music. Gillespie felt as though he could sit at the window and listen to them all night.

Eventually, Dizzy lifted the trumpet to his lips and cut loose, adding his own soaring cry to the city's blare. He had made up his mind. He would stick by his music no matter what it took.

Later that night, Gillespie put on his sharpest suit—pinstripes, wide lapels, baggy pants—and again made the rounds of New York's night spots. He covered the city by subway and visited a dozen clubs by sunrise. The tour dazzled him. Musicians he had heard on the radio since he was a child crowded tiny bandstands in smoky rooms, competing to play the best solos: Lester Young and Ben Webster on saxo-phone; Art Tatum burning up the keys on piano; Charlie Christian plucking quick, sweet notes on guitar. And at last, Gillespie's true hero, trumpeter Roy Eldridge, who could play as fast, it seemed, as a saxophonist, joyously rolling cascades of notes from the bell of his horn.

Gillespie noticed how the musicians pushed and encouraged each other to try something they had not heard before. All of these smoky little nightclubs were like laboratories where popular songs were twisted into new shapes, where their trite phrases were wrung for meaning and power no one could have guessed they possessed.

For weeks, Gillespie practiced his trumpet during the day. At night, he carried it to all the nightclubs and tried to get himself invited onstage. Opportuni-ties soon arose, and he rapidly earned a reputation as a promising soloist in the style of Roy Eldridge. Gillespie seemed wild on horn, but what he lacked in control he made up for in speed and exuberance. Some of the older musicians even claimed to hear a

The fast-fingered Roy Eldridge, who left the Teddy Hill Orchestra's horn section in 1937. According to Gillespie, the trumpeter who replaced Eldridge, "The real reason Teddy hired me, I believe, was because I sounded so much like Roy."

new idea or two in the way he phrased his solos.

On nights when Gillespie was not playing jam sessions at the small clubs, he waited at the door of the Savoy Ballroom on Lenox Avenue in Harlem. This was the premier dance hall in the country. Live radio broadcasts spread the big-band music played there into living rooms coast to coast.

Gillespie could not afford a ticket to go inside, so he stood at the door to glimpse the Lindy Hop dancers and to hear the house band, the Savoy Sultans. As he later wrote in his autobiography, *To Be or Not to Bop*, the Sultans "had enough rhythm for a thousand piece orchestra." When the band swung into a tune, women leaped into the air and, with their skirts flying, sailed between their partners' legs, over their backs, and onto the floor to spin and leap again.

The doorman at the Savoy eventually took pity on the young man with the trumpet and let Gillespie slip inside without paying. Dizzy learned the smoothest steps of all the dances in no time. Between sets, he stood near the bandstand and tried to get the Chick Webb Orchestra, the Savoy Sultans— whatever band was playing—to invite him onstage. Sometimes, when there was room, he would be allowed to join the trumpet section for a few songs. Then it was *his* music sailing across America by radio waves, spurring on a nation of dancers.

Long after sunrise, Gillespie would stumble back to his brother's apartment with a few dollars in his pocket—a bonus for playing at the Savoy. These occasions left him convinced that he had made the right choice to stick with his music.

One night when Gillespie played at the Savoy Ballroom, bandleader Teddy Hill arrived backstage. Gillespie's hero, Roy Eldridge, was about to leave the Teddy Hill Orchestra, and the bandleader wanted to find a replacement who played in Eldridge's breathless style. Hill knew he had found his man when Gillespie stood for a solo. The bandleader walked over to Dizzy between songs and asked if he would like to make $70 a week—a whopping sum in those days— by joining his orchestra on an upcoming tour of Europe.

Gillespie grabbed Hill's hand quickly, before the bandleader could change his mind. As Dizzy recalled later, "I was 20 years old, single, and insane." Hill did not have to ask twice.

Gillespie was, in fact, still 19, and because he was under the legal age, he had to get his mother's signature to acquire a passport. Nevertheless, he was now making it on his own. Dizzy celebrated his good luck by buying fashionable new clothes, signing up

for trumpet classes, and treating his brother to hearty dinners.

But success would never go to Gillespie's head. He spent every spare moment rehearsing, exploring new musical routes on the piano and coaxing ever more complex melodies from the songs he played. Some days he almost captured on his trumpet the riotous sounds he heard on the street. He understood, however, that it would take diligent practice, spectacular skill, and some measure of luck and genius to pour all that soulful energy into a single horn.

Featuring odd offbeats and difficult phrasings, Gillespie's high-energy jazz clashed with the smooth-flowing swing music favored by bandleader Teddy Hill (far left) and his orchestra. Horn section leader Bill Dillard, for one, admitted that Gillespie's "whole conception of playing trumpet and what he was trying to achieve was foreign to me."

Gillespie's constant experimentation soon got on the nerves of some members of the Teddy Hill Orchestra. These musicians had settled into their job like businessmen. They knew the tunes, played them, picked up their paychecks, and went home. The young dynamo in the trumpet section ruffled their feathers.

At last, the veteran band members asked for a meeting with Hill to air their complaints. Hiring such a young trumpeter cheapened their act, they said. Gillespie's speedy solos, wrung from growling low notes to shattering highs, clashed with their smooth-flowing sound. How could anybody dance to something like that? And if that was not enough, the man was a clown. Behind the bandleader's back, he made faces, threw spitballs, and waved at the audience.

Then the group of band members delivered their ultimatum: If Hill did not fire Gillespie before their trip to Europe, they would quit.

Hill listened to their complaints, trying hard to hide a smile. He knew they were bluffing. Besides, he liked the way the new kid shook up the older men and kept them on their toes. In fact, Gillespie's constant rehearsing and experimentation set a good example for his elders. He recorded two solos with the band in May 1937, and when the *Ile de France* ocean liner sailed out of New York Harbor in June, Hill saw to it that Dizzy Gillespie and his trumpet were on board.

All the way to Europe, the ship seemed like a giant dance hall. Along with the orchestra came the entire revue from New York's celebrated Cotton Club, including a dozen chorus girls, a dozen tap dancers, and a bluesy tramp band, which played piano, washboard, and kazoos. The only person missing from the original troupe was the Cotton Club's biggest star, singer and bandleader Cab Calloway.

As the colorful youngest member of the Teddy Hill Orchestra, Gillespie became the darling of the women on board. In his spare time, he studied music with Bill Dillard, the leader of the orchestra's trumpet section. Dillard reminded the young musician that improvising a solo could be like dancing or flirting or anything else: A pause in the right place or one long, sustained note was a more effective way to make the audience swoon than an overpowering assault of flashy notes. This was a lesson Gillespie never forgot.

The first stop on the three-month tour was Paris. The orchestra performed at the Moulin Rouge, a fashionable nightclub on le boulevard de Clichy. Most of the French patrons had never heard a big swing band play live, but they were quickly won over by the deft rhythms and driving power of the ensemble. Record producers scrambled to sign up individual band members, but somehow nobody asked Gillespie, who was in his formative years as a jazz innovator, to make a record.

So Gillespie roamed the streets, just as he had done in New York, taking in all the sights and sounds, from the Eiffel Tower to the city's imposing

A fashionably dressed Gillespie—"Cats still remember that green tweed coat from England," he said—on a London street during his 1937 European tour with the Teddy Hill Orchestra. The most celebrated item of clothing he bought on the trip was a beret, which through his example became the trademark hat of jazz lovers.

cathedrals. It was in Paris that he purchased his first beret, which through his example would become the favorite hat of jazz lovers everywhere. He rounded out his new look by sauntering into rehearsals sporting a long-stemmed cigarette holder, determined not to let the stuffy older guys ruin his good times.

Onstage, Gillespie's comic impersonations of other band members amused the audience and won him some new friends in the orchestra. Yet Teddy Hill began to wonder at the same time whether hiring the young trumpeter had been a good idea after all. Gillespie never seemed comfortable with the basic swing rhythm; he always tried to change the tempo, interjecting odd offbeats and difficult phrasings that threw the other musicians off. Sometimes, when he tried one of his soaring wild solos, he got lost. But instead of shrinking away in embarrassment, he just grinned and shook his head, then tried an even more difficult solo the next time. By the time the tour ended, with stops in England and Ireland, Hill had taken away most of Gillespie's solo opportunities.

When Gillespie returned to the United States in the fall of 1937, he went straight to Philadelphia to give his mother some of the money he had earned. Then he came back to New York, all set to pick up where he had left off. Instead, he found out he could not rejoin the Teddy Hill Orchestra right away. Now that he was a steady member of a band, he needed to have a union card. It took three months for the permit to be issued.

In the meantime, Gillespie performed without the band, jamming at after-hours clubs with pianist Edgar Hayes and others. These jobs paid poorly, however, and he was soon running low on cash, just as he had during his first visit to New York. Then his situation went from bad to worse: J.P. moved out of the apartment they had been sharing. Left to fend for himself, the young jazzman who had dazzled the crowds in Paris weeks earlier was reduced to bumming 15 cents on the street to buy a bowl of soup.

"Those were pretty hard times," Gillespie recalled, "but I never even considered taking another kind of job. Hell no! I was going to make my living as a musician, even though I wasn't making any money."

Once again, he rehearsed all day, often on an empty stomach, and visited the clubs at night. The chorus girls laughed at him when he came around. They expected jazz musicians to have lots of money, and Gillespie was flat broke.

One of the chorus girls at Harlem's Apollo Theatre took pity on him, though. A petite young dancer named Lorraine Willis, she occasionally bought him a sandwich or some soup. Before long, Gillespie began to slip notes to her backstage, asking for a date. But Willis was not one to play around. She saved her paycheck, went home right after each show, and stayed out of trouble. Even after they began dating, Gillespie rarely got to see her for more than half an hour between performances.

Gillespie's union card finally arrived in early 1938, and with it came a deluge of job offers. He signed with the Savoy Sultans as well as with the Teddy Hill Orchestra. After hours, he played in a Latin band led by Cuban-born flutist Alberto Soccares.

In Latin bands, which featured lively conga and rhumba tunes, the drummers played all sorts of rhythms, and the other musicians added new rhythms on top of them. The result was a busy, vibrant sound that allowed a trumpeter more freedom than when he played with a swing orchestra. In Soccares's Latin band, Gillespie was able, for the first time in his career, to cut loose with his intricate, fiery phrasing without fear of angering the bandleader. If only there

Drummer Kenny Clarke's ability to act as a true accompanist "furnished just the right amount of support, push, or embellishment I needed," Gillespie said. The two musicians formed their close working relationship in 1939, while they were playing with the Teddy Hill Orchestra.

was some way to bring all those polyrhythms, all that freedom, into the music of a swing band!

Gillespie's dream began to come true in 1939, when a 25-year-old drummer named Kenny Clarke joined the Teddy Hill Orchestra. Instead of keeping regular time with the bass drum, Clarke kept the beat with a light touch on the cymbals. Meanwhile, he played another rhythm on the snare drums and used a foot pedal to "drop bombs" here and there on the bass drum.

Clarke (nicknamed Klook-Mop for the sound of his drums) drummed in a totally new way, and it drove the older musicians crazy. To Gillespie, however, Clarke's playing came as a revelation: Here was a guy who played drums the same way he himself played trumpet!

The two outcasts immediately became friends. They learned each other's parts, worked out new drum and trumpet figures on the piano, and talked constantly of bringing the churning sound of the modern city into their playing. With Gillespie's encouragement, Clarke revolutionized jazz drumming, proving that a percussionist could do more than just keep time. Clarke became a true accompanist, providing clever accents for soloists and propelling the whole band with sprightly rhythms that seemed spontaneous.

Gillespie realized right away that they were on the track of something big. When the brassy tones of his trumpet and Klook-Mop's cymbals blended, they created a new sound, a young person's music full of excitement and surprise. If he could only round up enough bandmates like Kenny Clarke, they might turn the jazz world on its ear.

Dizzy Gillespie had never shrunk from a challenge before, and nothing would stop him now. ❧

2

"MISCHIEF, MONEY-MAKING, AND MUSIC"

Dizzy—christened John Birks—and his brother Wesley (left) standing near their home in Cheraw, South Carolina. John was the youngest of the nine Gillespie children.

IT TOOK COURAGE and self-confidence for a teenage trumpet player to move to New York City in search of work with a top swing band. It took raw talent, concentration, and steadfast humor to make a place for himself among the jealous fraternity of older musicians in such a band. And above all, it took an iron will and unshakable ambition to challenge the rules in search of a new way of making music. Dizzy Gillespie possessed all these qualities in abundance, qualities that began to make themselves evident while he was still a child.

Dizzy Gillespie, christened John Birks, was born in the small town of Cheraw, South Carolina, on October 21, 1917. "My arrival probably didn't excite anybody," he wrote in *To Be or Not to Bop*. "So many people had been born at our house before." He was James and Lottie Gillespie's ninth and last child. Seven of them—Edward, Mattie, James (J.P.), Hattie Marie, Eugenia, Wesley, and John—lived past childbirth.

The Gillespies' house sat along a dirt road beside similar wood-frame homes that clustered together beneath the enormous blue sky, surrounded on all sides by broad cotton fields. Everyone in the neighborhood drew water in buckets from a well located next to one of the three local black churches.

James Gillespie worked hard as a brickmason and builder to support his large family. But his first love was music, and whenever an opportunity came along, he toured the Eastern Seaboard to play the piano with a dance band.

When at home, James Gillespie demanded obedience from his children and exacted it with a leather razor strop. Young John would cringe in his bed whenever his father called his name. "Every Sunday morning, Papa would whip us," Gillespie wrote in his autobiography. "That's mainly how I remember him. . . . He was usually mean; and he hated to see or hear about his children misbehaving."

Two of the Gillespie boys, Edward and J.P., ran away from home when they were teenagers to escape their father's wrath. As the youngest member of the family, John could only crawl out of bed and take his punishment. In later years, however, he tried to make sense of his father's angry temper, reckoning that "he treated us that way because he wanted us all to be tough and he turned me into a tough little rebel, very early, against everyone but him."

James Gillespie never had the time or the inclination to teach his children music, but they grew up surrounded by musical instruments he had picked up during his travels. In the living room sat an upright piano, a guitar, a set of drums, a mandolin, and even a big red one-string bass fiddle. Most of the older kids considered these instruments junk, but John loved them. He imagined that these toys of wood and string could make wonderful music in the proper hands, like the tunes that wafted in the windows from his next-door neighbor's radio.

The Gillespies could not afford their own radio or phonograph, so John spent countless hours next door, in Amanda Harrington's living room, thrilling to broadcasts of big-band jazz from magical places such as the Savoy Ballroom. The rich voices of the announcers, the suave tones of the singers, and the overwhelming power of a 20-piece band at full throttle evoked a magical world of fancy clothes and easy living far from the sandy fields and razor strops of the Gillespies' neighborhood.

At the same time, the music made John want to jump about and dance, and he could see that it moved other listeners, too. Amanda Harrington tapped her feet and grinned during the fast numbers. When a vocalist such as the incomparable Bessie Smith sang a sad tune, the former schoolteacher wiped tears from her eyes.

John discovered similarly powerful music in church. His family belonged to the local Methodist church, where hymns were performed solemnly. Down the road by the well, at the Sanctified Congregation, however, he knew that people leaped about and wailed gospel tunes with unbridled passion whenever the spirit moved them. He often sneaked into one of the rear pews and listened in wonder and amazement to the evening services.

Meanwhile, John seemed to take the brunt of the punishment at home. His brothers and sisters ganged up on their baby brother, and Lottie Gillespie, with her hands full trying to feed such a huge family, could only shrug her shoulders when he complained. There was only one thing left to do. He had to learn to stand up for himself.

So, very early in his life, John began to display the resourcefulness by which he is known to this day. On the outside, he developed a happy-go-lucky personality that could disarm a troublemaker with a joke or a smile. On the inside, he hid a mean streak that matched his father's.

By the time he entered Robert Smalls Public School in 1922, the whole neighborhood knew that anyone who picked on little John Birks had to expect a fight. He would come at them with arms flailing,

The trumpeter's parents, James and Lottie Gillespie, on their front steps in Cheraw. John inherited his love of music from his father, a brickmason and builder who played in a band on weekends and whose hobby was collecting musical instruments.

legs kicking, throwing sticks and stones. "I spent a lot of time getting into mischief in class," he acknowledged.

John was 10 years old when his father died suddenly one morning of an asthma attack. Stunned, the youngster responded the only way he knew how. As he recalled years later, "Anger got control of me after Papa died and instead of grieving I became real mean and used to do all kinds of devilish things." One schoolmate, Buddy Sharper, made the mistake of suggesting that James Gillespie had gone to hell. John almost killed him in a fight. He bullied younger kids, teased the slow ones, and started battles with bigger boys that his brother Wesley had to break up.

Keeping John out of trouble and interested in his schoolwork could wear a teacher out. Fortunately, his music teacher, Alice Wilson, stumbled on a solution. At the end of each year, she put together a student minstrel show, complete with music, comedy, and drama. In 1929, she handed John a beat-up trombone and challenged him to play it. In doing so, she discovered the key to his heart. Although his arms were too short to move the trombone's slide very far, he practiced every day. He even came to school with the horn under his arm. Wilson was amazed at the way an old trombone soothed her wildest student, who would not sit still during class but would spend hours after school concentrating on his music.

One winter day, while John practiced his trombone at home, a similar yet higher tone sounded from next door. He ran immediately to the Harringtons' house and discovered Amanda Harrington's son, Brother, holding on to his latest Christmas present: a brand-new nickel-plated trumpet. Already, the boy knew how to play the B-flat scale, pumping the valves like a showman. John could hardly wait to give it a try.

From that day on, the two youngsters practiced together. And within a few months, 12-year-old John amazed Alice Wilson once again: He could now play not one but two instruments with ease. When the time came for the annual minstrel show, she put together a small band to accompany the singers and dancers. By then, John had completed the switch from his trombone to a cornet, which resembles a trumpet.

Meanwhile, money had grown scarce at the Gillespie home. After the death of her husband, Lottie Gillespie tried to earn a living by taking in laundry, but the money she made was not enough to feed her large family. So, even though jobs were few and far between in Cheraw, all of the Gillespie children looked for work.

John considered himself fortunate to find a job guarding the door of a movie house. The pay amounted to very little, but the owner let him watch

A view of Gillespie's birthplace—the poor rural town of Cheraw—in the mid-1910s. Like most of the black families residing in northeast South Carolina, the Gillespies, Dizzy said, "never had to worry about being spoiled by riches."

Alice Wilson, Gillespie's third-grade teacher and first music instructor, standing in front of the Robert Smalls Public School in Cheraw. She became "my mentor," the trumpeter said, "and, later, the greatest early influence in my development as a musician."

all the movies for free. John especially loved the westerns, starring Tom Mix, the Lone Ranger, and other screen heroes. Sometimes, the show included a short jazz film. The sight of the glamorous Duke Ellington Orchestra—with all the musicians in white tuxedos and the suave Duke himself counting off the numbers with a snap of his fingers—dazzled the budding musician.

John earned some extra cash at a local whites-only swimming pool. Like most communities in the South, Cheraw was a racially segregated town, with Jim Crow laws leading to separate facilities for blacks and whites. Fearlessly, John performed swan dives and half gainers from the high diving board, recovering the pennies and nickels the patrons had thrown into the pool as his reward. He also picked cotton with his brothers, but he hated the work and swore he would find a better way to make a living. More and more, he began to think that music might be the key.

After the school year ended in 1930, John continued to rehearse with the student minstrel band over the summer. He played a taped-up cornet, and Bill McNeil, who was tall enough to play the slide easily, took over on trombone. Other classmates dropped in from time to time, adding their skills on clarinet, bass violin, and saxophone.

John's favorite bandmate was Wes Buchanan, who could get all sorts of subtle or stomping rhythms going on just a single bass drum. Sometimes, he beat the drum like a tom-tom with his hands; occasionally, he rested an elbow on the skin to dampen the sound. According to Gillespie, who has always favored innovative drummers, Buchanan's raw talent has never been matched.

Before the summer ended, the little minstrel band developed a steady following at local house parties. They performed rollicking tunes with titles such as "I Can't Dance, I Got Ants in My Pants" and "Wild Goose Chase." John often leaped into the crowd to perform his slinky version of a dance called the snake hips while the audience cleared a space for him and tossed money on the floor. All that fun made it clear to the youngest Gillespie why his father had loved music so much. As the trumpet player said in his autobiography, "In Cheraw, mischief, money-making, and music captured all of my attention."

John's confidence soared when the band teacher at the local white high school invited him to teach rhythm and timing to the students. Their instruments were shiny and new, but they listened attentively when the skinny black youngster, still in elementary school, burst into a fast-paced cadenza on his taped-up cornet.

But just when John thought he knew everything about music, he was taught a cruel lesson that he has never forgotten. Sonny Matthews, a local youth who had been attending school out of state, returned to Cheraw, trumpet in hand. He wasted no time in seeking out the new horn man he had heard so much about.

When the two finally met, Matthews launched into a tune in the key of C and invited Gillespie to join in. The music that Matthews played sounded easy to perform, yet John could not find a single note on his cornet that sounded right with it. He could only shake his head and admit he was lost. His music teacher had only taught her students to play in the key of B-flat. Matthews laughed and strolled out of the room, having bested his rival with one tune.

John did not suffer defeat gladly. He suddenly realized that there existed a whole world of music he had not known about, and he quizzed the band teacher at the white high school, professional musicians who passed through town, and anybody else he could find to explain it to him. Within a few months, he and his bandmates had mastered the ability to perform in several keys.

But John was not content to let the issue rest. Vowing that he would never again be embarrassed by the likes of Sonny Matthews, he experimented constantly with new ideas about playing harmonies. In fact, the main innovation he brought to the musical style he later helped create—bebop—was the way he improvised in different keys, enabling him to create exotic new melodies at the speed of thought. By the time he was an adult, no trumpet player in the world could beat Gillespie at harmonic improvisation. So in this way, a simple incident between schoolboys in Cheraw, South Carolina, may ultimately have led to a revolution in American music.

While he was still a youth, John made so much progress on his cornet that when a touring professional band came through town, he was sometimes allowed to join in for a few tunes. According to his brother Wesley, "People were wild about him because they knew that he had talent." Standing on a box so the dancers could see him, John played his heart out on his old, taped-up cornet. At night, he continued to sit in front of the radio next door, listening to the Teddy Hill Orchestra, with its premier trumpet man, Roy Eldridge, wow the crowds in New York City. John dreamed of joining such a group someday, but even he could not have imagined that before he reached the age of 20 he would replace Eldridge in that same band.

John graduated from Robert Smalls in 1933. The ninth-grader spent that summer with Wesley as a laborer on a road construction crew. John, however, hated shoveling dirt as much as he disliked picking cotton. All around him were men who would go on breaking their back at some tedious, low-paying job for the rest of their life. He spent every waking hour trying to figure out how to stay out of that ditch.

The future jazz master at age 17. According to one of Gillespie's teachers, "He would come to school every morning with his horn under his arm, instead of books."

At the end of the summer, Catherine McKay, a neighbor who worked as a nurse at the Laurinburg Technical Institute, offered John a remarkable opportunity. She told him that Laurinburg, a private school for exceptional high school students, could use a new trumpet player in its band. The school would be willing to admit young Gillespie if he promised to study hard and stay out of trouble.

John leaped for joy when he found out it would not cost him a penny to attend Laurinburg. As he recalled in *To Be or Not to Bop*, "I only had one shirt to my name, no money for tuition, no really great desire to be educated, and didn't even own a trumpet. I went to Laurinburg Technical Institute strictly on my own lips. They gave me food, tuition, room, books, and everything else I needed, free."

John arrived at Laurinburg, which was located about 30 miles across the border in North Carolina, in September. The school was set amid green farmland and had plenty of buildings; to John, it seemed like a self-contained small town. He immediately tried out for the football team, even though he was smaller than most of the other boys. He overcame his lack of size with fearless play and made the squad as an offensive end—he even scored Laurinburg's very first touchdown.

John played football for only one season, however. When an opposing player, aware of Gillespie's trumpet prowess, threatened to knock his teeth out, the young musician reconsidered his place on the team; he had to protect his mouth so he could play the trumpet. Eventually, John decided to make a sacrifice for his music. He told the coach he would not be playing football the following season.

John discovered early on that none of his teachers at Laurinburg knew more about music than he did. Disappointed, he chose to practice on his own, playing both the piano and the trumpet late into the night. "I developed a very serious attitude about music," he recalled, "and music was the only thing I was serious about." On the weekends, he performed at dances with his friends from Cheraw.

John now felt that he had saved himself from becoming a construction laborer. Then Bill McNeil disappeared suddenly; he was rumored to have been lynched by racist whites. John realized that life on a road gang was not the only horrible fate awaiting a poor black man in the South, and he decided to get out of Cheraw as soon as he got the chance.

John was a high school junior in 1935 when his family moved to Philadelphia, where his mother's sister lived. Like thousands of other rural blacks in the 1930s, the Gillespies believed that better opportunities existed in the big industrial cities of the

North. Mattie and Eugenia landed jobs doing piece-work at a sewing factory, and Wesley found work as a cook in a restaurant. That summer, even though he was just a year away from graduating, John dropped out of Laurinburg and caught a train north to join them.

The Gillespie clan now crowded into a three-and-a-half-room apartment at 637 Pine Street. They were determined to make a better life for themselves than they had known in South Carolina. And the youngest of them held the grandest dreams of all.

Within three days of his arrival, John landed a job as a trumpeter with a local swing band, and within six months he had joined the Frankie Fairfax Band. Impatient for a new musical challenge, he moved to New York City before the year was out and eventually found a position with the Teddy Hill Orchestra.

In a very short time, John Birks—now nicknamed Dizzy—Gillespie had pulled himself out of a life of certain drudgery as a poor black laborer in South Carolina. He did it with a rare combination of musical talent, a fierce determination that bordered on orneriness, and a willingness to take a chance for something better at every step. He would further test these qualities in the years ahead as he set out to revolutionize the world of music. ◀◉▶

3

REBEL WITHOUT A PAUSE

CHAFING AT THE limits of swing, Dizzy Gillespie and Kenny Clarke worked together to overcome these constraints after they met in New York City in 1939. As they began to sort out their new musical ideas at jam sessions in small Harlem clubs, their reputation as rebels grew. "Only a few people understood what was going on," Clarke said. "Everybody knew it was good, but they couldn't figure out what it was."

One musician who was impressed by the young rebels was Gillespie's former jam-session partner Edgar Hayes. When the Teddy Hill Orchestra broke up because of a union dispute in 1939, both Gillespie and Clarke joined Hayes's group. The piano-playing bandleader allowed the adventurous young musicians more leeway with their experiments than Teddy Hill had.

"He loved his music," Hayes later said of Gillespie. "He'd sit up there with his horn all the time. He'd always have his horn ready to fill in on something."

Trumpeter Carl Warwick, one of Gillespie's former colleagues from Philadelphia, was already a member of Hayes's band. Warwick marveled at the progress his friend Dizzy had made in just a couple of years. At one jam session in Harlem, the speed and dexterity of Gillespie's improvisations even surprised his longtime hero, Roy Eldridge.

"I was always doing my damndest to be hip," Gillespie said of his early years on the jazz scene, especially when he was with the Cab Calloway Orchestra. The trumpeter claimed, for example, that on the bandstand, "I used to sing, 'I'm Diz the Wiz, a swinging hip cat. Swinging hip cat, Diz the Wiz.' Then Cab would say something, and then I played."

Despite the freedom afforded by Hayes, work with his band was not all that steady. Pretty soon Gillespie began to look for a better-paying job with a larger swing band. Extra money would come in handy because he and Lorraine Willis were thinking of getting married.

Good fortune came in the guise of trumpeter Mario Bauza, whom Gillespie had befriended several years earlier at the Savoy. Bauza was now playing with one of the classiest big bands around, the Cab Calloway Orchestra. According to Gillespie, "Cab Calloway's band was the big leagues for a black musician. The money was good, and the traveling was easy."

Calloway had never heard of Gillespie, so Bauza came up with a scheme for his friend to play his way into the band. One night during an engagement at the Cotton Club, Bauza gave his uniform to Gillespie and told him to take his place onstage. Dizzy did just that. As he remembers it, "I tore up one number, 'Cuban Nightmare,' a Latin type thing," and he kept the dancers hopping all night. Calloway liked what he heard and offered Gillespie a spot with the band for $80 a week.

Gillespie had never seen such a splendid-looking outfit as the Cab Calloway Orchestra. The musicians all wore fashionable double-breasted zoot suits with long coats that reached halfway to the knee. They traveled by private railroad car and brought with them an entourage that could make any stage in the country seem as though it were the home of a Broadway show. Those who came along as part of the Cab Calloway production were singer Avis Andrews; Moke 'n' Poke, a comedy duo; three male tap dancers, the Chocolateers; and six more dancers, the Cotton Club Boys. To make such an elaborate show work, Calloway insisted on strict discipline. Everyone had to look sharp, be on time, and be ready to play at every stop.

Gillespie respected Calloway for his insistence on punctuality and performance, yet it was part of Dizzy's nature to act the clown. He could not resist committing practical jokes on his bandmates or mugging at the audience. Calloway, one of the most expressive singers in American music, might be crooning a mellow love song at the front of the stage and could not figure out why the audience would be breaking into laughter. What he failed to see was his young trumpeter pretending to pass an imaginary football across the stage to the saxophone player, who received Gillespie's toss just as the drummer hit the bass drum for punctuation.

Hijinks such as that drove the perfectionist bandleader crazy. If that was not enough, Gillespie continued to experiment with harmonies, shooting off in impossible directions during his solos. His bandmates would look on, bug eyed, at his daring. Calloway, from his place at the front of the stage, would turn around to the trumpet section and frown at the way Dizzy broke up the rhythm with "that Chinese music." To the bandleader, Gillespie's rough playing ruined the elegant sound of his orchestra.

Nevertheless, Calloway could not deny Gillespie's unique talent. The bandleader featured the young trumpeter as a soloist both in concert and on records.

One of Gillespie's earliest recorded appearances came on a tune called "Pluckin' the Bass," an up-tempo vehicle for bassist Milt Hinton. Gillespie had been working with Hinton on the roof of the Cotton Club after hours, showing him the rhythmic innovations he had worked out with Kenny Clarke in the Teddy Hill Orchestra. Hinton put these lessons to good use in "Pluckin' the Bass," plucking and slapping the strings in rapid alternation. Gillespie's solo in the song shows that at age 22 he was already developing a distinct and original voice.

Then, on a song Gillespie wrote himself, "Pickin'

the Cabbage," he tested ideas that he would spend the rest of his career developing. "It's a real beginning of Latin jazz and possibly the first use of polyrhythms in our music since the very beginning of jazz," he noted. "All of the elements for fusing and synthesizing Afro-American 'swing' with the various Latin and Caribbean beats are right there in that one composition."

Before long, Gillespie's performances—both live and on records—had won him fans across the country. "He really filled the bill, being a fine musician," Calloway said, "and added as much, or more, to my band as anybody." By 1940, Gillespie was known to just about everybody as Diz the Wiz.

Cab Calloway (far left) conducts his orchestra, which included Gillespie (back row, left) on trumpet, during a 1940 radio broadcast. "It was the best job that you could possibly have, high class," Gillespie said of his position with the big band.

That same year, he met a musician who was every bit the wizard that Gillespie was. Dizzy was touring with the Cab Calloway Orchestra in St. Louis when fellow trumpeter Buddy Anderson introduced him to 20-year-old Charlie Parker. An alto saxophone player, Parker was known as Yardbird (or Bird, for short) and played with the Jay McShann Orchestra. It was only a matter of time before Bird showed Dizzy a thing or two.

One night after the Cab Calloway Orchestra ended one of its shows, Gillespie, Parker, and Anderson found a piano in a vacant room and began to fool around on it. Dizzy knew instantly that Bird was a musician to be reckoned with. "I never heard any-

Twenty-year-old saxophonist Charlie Parker (left) was a member of the Jay McShann Orchestra when he first met Gillespie in 1940. The two musicians soon joined forces and revolutionized the jazz world.

thing like that before," Gillespie recalled years later. "The way that he assembled notes together. This was one of the greatest thrills because I had been a Roy Eldridge fan up until then, but I was definitely moving on into myself. Charlie Parker and I were moving in practically the same direction, too, but neither of us knew it."

The two men would not meet again for two years. But when they did, fireworks went off that would dazzle music lovers worldwide.

In the meantime, Gillespie continued to tour with the Cab Calloway Orchestra. While he was performing in Pittsburgh, he received his draft notice from the U.S. Army. He left the band and returned to New York in early 1940 to undergo a physical examination.

Gillespie wanted no part of the military, which was then racially segregated. He arrived for the physical carrying his trumpet under his arm. When he was told to strip off his clothes, he complied, yet he continued to hold on to his horn. Gillespie, of course, was an old hand at acting "dizzy."

When he was asked about his views on shooting the enemy, Gillespie expressed more of a willingness to fight people who were bigoted than to shoot the enemy. The army psychiatrists kept him under observation for a few days. Then they pronounced him "unfit for service."

Freed from his military obligation, Gillespie rejoined the Calloway band. He learned new rhythmic variations from bandmate Mario Bauza and worked with Milt Hinton on developing unusual accents and fills. Gradually, he wove these more sophisticated improvisations into the tightly structured Cab Calloway sound.

Calloway's orchestra was in Boston that spring when Gillespie finally popped the question to his sweetheart, Lorraine, who was in town that same weekend. They were married on May 9, 1940, by a justice of the peace. Then, like the troupers they were, they separated again as Gillespie hit the road.

It had to be a difficult time for the young couple, trying to establish their marriage across long distances. But the Gillespies had more in common than a love of show business. Lorraine had been born in New York, but she had spent her summers growing up with her grandmother in Darlington, South Carolina, not far from Dizzy's hometown. The newlyweds understood each other well. Like her husband, Lorraine had developed an unshakable determination to fight for those things in which she believed. By sheer force of will, she made a home for them in New York and taught Dizzy to save his money, as she saved hers. This marriage, built on the unsteady ground of touring bands, would last.

Whenever the Calloway band performed in New York City, Gillespie sought out his old bandmate Kenny Clarke. Klook-Mop had again found work with Teddy Hill, this time at the club the former bandleader managed, a tiny place called Minton's Playhouse, on 118th Street in Harlem. Clarke introduced Gillespie to the house pianist, a shy bear of a man with the unforgettable name Thelonius Monk. Gillespie instantly recognized that Monk shared his vision of a polyrhythmic music in which the harmony would vary.

Sometimes when they were jamming together, Gillespie would lay down his trumpet and play the piano alongside Monk, with the two of them trying new variations on the keyboard until dawn. Clarke, who also played piano, would often sit in and add his ideas to the mix. Now Gillespie knew four musicians—Clarke, Monk, Milt Hinton, and Charlie Parker—who thought as he did. If the five of them ever got together, who could tell what wonders might evolve?

But for now Gillespie hit the road again; his lucrative job with Cab Calloway beckoned. Tensions arose, however, as Gillespie grew increasingly impatient with the stodgy arrangements and repetitive boredom of swing. Though he was always serious about his music, he could not resist clowning around both onstage and off. When other band members joined in with *their* hijinks, Calloway began to feel he was losing control of the band he had so carefully groomed to represent the essence of New York style and refinement to cities all over the country.

The last straw fell at the State Theatre in Hartford in 1941. Most of the orchestra waited backstage while Calloway danced out front to the music of the Cab Jivers, a five-piece ensemble made up of his favorite bandmates. This small group provided one of the more intimate moments in

"She gives me the anchor that I need," Gillespie said of former chorus-line dancer Lorraine Willis, to whom he has been married for more than 50 years.

Calloway's show; the elegant instrumental solos complemented his slinky soft-shoe dancing and sly vocals. It was during such a moment that the bandleader turned around, just in time to see a big, sopping spitball plop at his feet.

Calloway finished up the show, then stormed backstage, raving about the insult. There was no doubt in his mind who the culprit was. It had to be that irreverent sprite, Dizzy Gillespie.

Pianist Thelonius Monk was among the most innovative musicians with whom Gillespie jammed in the early 1940s. "Our influence on one another's music is so closely related that Monk doesn't actually know what I showed him," Gillespie said. "But I do know some of the things that he showed me."

The bandleader stopped Gillespie the instant he saw him and began yelling. A surprised Dizzy replied that he had not thrown the spitball. Calloway would have none of that. To press his point in front of the entire band, he grabbed Gillespie by his coat lapels and shouted into his face that he was a liar.

Calloway had made an unfortunate miscalculation. Perhaps he was unaware that since the age of six Gillespie had been bravely taking on all comers. Perhaps he had not heard the story about the South Philly youths who had tried to drag young Dizzy into their car, only to retreat after he nearly sliced off the hand of one passenger with a knife he carried in his pocket. Whatever the case, Gillespie issued just one warning. "I didn't do it," he told the bandleader. "Take your hands off me."

"I say you did it," Calloway replied. "Now, go ahead on, or else I'll slap you down."

Gillespie looked coldly into the eyes of the taller man. "You ain't gonna do nothing."

With that, Calloway's hand rose and slapped Gillespie's face. Before it could drop to his side, the trumpet player had whipped out a knife and sliced through the bandleader's expensive white trousers, cutting him along the hip and thigh. As blood began to spread down Calloway's suit, Milt Hinton jumped forward and wrestled the knife out of Gillespie's hand.

Calloway could not believe what had happened. Even before he taped up his wound, he demanded that Gillespie pack his bags and leave. "Get him outta here!" the bandleader yelled to the onlookers.

It was not until years later that the truth came out about who had thrown the fateful spitball. Calloway was right that it had come from the trumpet section. The real culprit, however, was a player named Jonah Jones.

In later years, Gillespie would realize that his stint with the Cab Calloway Orchestra had provided him with the security he had needed to develop his own musical style. Calloway had also taught him a lot about showmanship, about running a band, and even about scat singing—the stringing together of nonsense syllables to carry the rhythm of a tune. Calloway specialized in this form of singing, but Gillespie would soon make it his own.

For now, though, the angry young trumpeter found himself back on the street, newly married, and suddenly lacking that high-paying job with the swankiest big band in America. He took a train to New York City that night and homed in immediately on Minton's Playhouse, the little Harlem club in which his true soulmates had set up shop.

For some people, bad luck provides an opportunity. Dizzy Gillespie has always been one of those people. In after-hours jam sessions over the next two years, he and his self-described oddball cohorts would invent a whole new sound that was unlike anything anyone had ever heard. The revolution called bebop had begun. ❧

4

THE MAGIC AT MINTON'S

Dizzy GILLESPIE RETURNED to New York City in 1941 determined to get three things: "payment, respect, and recognition." With these goals in mind, he stormed through 11 of the most important bands in the country in a single year. He played in the orchestras of Ella Fitzgerald, Coleman Hawkins, Benny Carter, Charlie Barnet, Les Hite, Lucky Millinder, Claude Hopkins, Fess Williams, Calvin Jackson, Boyd Raeburn, and Fletcher Henderson. All of these bandleaders knew about Gillespie's fight with Cab Calloway, but they could not resist his unique talents.

Gillespie never settled for mere sideman status. He always demanded a chance to show his stuff and to be paid fairly. In addition, he began to write tunes at a remarkable rate, supplying the staid swing orchestras with more modern numbers to get the crowds hopping.

These stints provided Gillespie with a paycheck while he pursued his real work after hours. The big band shows ended by 11:00 P.M., and by the time the clock struck midnight he was on the bandstand at Minton's Playhouse, where he would jam with all

When former bandleader Teddy Hill (right) became manager of Minton's Playhouse, a New York City night spot, in 1941, he turned over the bandstand in the back room to (from left to right) Thelonius Monk, trumpeter Howard McGhee, Roy Eldridge, and other musicians who had worked for him. According to Gillespie, so much experimenting took place on the bandstand that "we had to be as sensitive to each other as brothers in order to express ourselves completely, maintain our individuality, yet play as one."

comers until dawn. It was there—and in a similar Harlem after-hours spot, Monroe's Uptown House—that modern jazz first took root.

Minton's was managed by Teddy Hill, the bandleader with whom Gillespie had toured Europe while still a teenager. Hill had fired drummer Kenny Clarke from his orchestra for playing in an unusual style, but he reconsidered his move when he took over at Minton's and hired Clarke to form a house band. Clarke brought in Thelonius Monk, a pianist whose shy, enigmatic manner belied his linebacker's physique, and these two men anchored a constantly changing lineup of musicians, all impatient to stretch the possibilities of their music to its limits.

Author Ralph Ellison was one of the many fans who crowded into Minton's at night, basking in the smoky veil of soft red light and the smells of fried chicken, sweat, and perfume. He said that the patrons "thought of Minton's as a sanctuary, where in the atmosphere blended of nostalgic and music-and-drink-lulled suspension of time they could retreat from the wartime tensions of the town."

For the musicians, Minton's meant even more. It was their playhouse, their diner, and their laboratory. Milt Hinton, Gillespie's friend from the Calloway band, lived directly across the street. Lorraine Gillespie had found an apartment nearby, at 2040 Seventh Avenue, above the rooms rented by drummer Shadow Wilson and singer Billy Eckstine. Minton's was where everyone met. They looked to the irrepressible Dizzy Gillespie for inspiration, and he did not let them down.

According to Kenny Clarke, Gillespie never seemed hampered by musical conventions. Instead of playing 3 notes in a chord, he tried to extend a chord by cramming 8, 9, even 11 notes into it. His motto was "Just try it." He urged drummers, bassists, pianists, and guitarists to give up their roles as keepers of the beat and risk improvising as full-fledged solo artists. The musicians jammed until dawn, then often piled into Gillespie's apartment.

While Lorraine fried up ham and eggs for the gang, Gillespie sat at his upright piano, working out new harmonies that could be transposed to the other instruments. Monk sat beside him, hammering out elliptical tunes, while Gillespie tapped his knee and hummed to show the drummers and horn men how to fit themselves into the music. (Gillespie himself was a decent drummer by this time, and modern masters such as Max Roach and Art Blakey later credited him with teaching them the new improvisational techniques.)

As more and more musicians sought out Minton's, the tiny bandstand grew crowded. Sometimes, as many as 30 horn men tried to wedge themselves onto the stage. It paid at such times to have taken part in the late-night sessions at Gillespie's apartment. To chase no-talent musicians off the bandstand, Gillespie and his friends would launch into their improvisational experiments. Few newcomers could keep up with them.

According to regular band member Joe Newman, "They'd say, 'Okay, you want to play so-and-so?' So the guys would put it in a key maybe like an F-sharp or something, anything where the fingering doesn't lay right on the horn. Everything you touch, it's not that, it's something else. And if you didn't really know your instrument and know the theory of music, you just don't play it. Every note you touch is wrong."

These attempts to drive musicians off the bandstand soon grew into something else entirely. Gillespie recalled that "after a while we got more and more interested in what we were doing as music, and, as we began to explore more and more, so our music evolved."

Gillespie sleeping on a train in 1943 between appearances with the Earl Hines Orchestra. He earned $20 a night by touring with the band.

Old masters such as saxophonists Lester Young and Coleman Hawkins often came by to test their prowess in highly competitive "cutting sessions." At one of these sessions, the Minton's gang realized it was truly on to something important. As Kenny Clarke remembers it, "One night after weeks of trying Dizzy cut [outplayed] Roy Eldridge. It was one night in many, but it meant a great deal. Roy had been top dog for years. We closed ranks after that."

Not all the young musicians who came to these cutting sessions were chased off by Gillespie and company. Charlie Parker came to town with the Jay McShann band, liked what he heard at Minton's, and promptly quit the orchestra so he could stay in New York. Already highly advanced in his technique, Parker quickly absorbed the new rhythmic and harmonic ideas and made himself known as a bright star in the after-hours clubs.

Gillespie, Parker, and the others worked hard at their music. With evening big-band jobs, jam sessions until dawn, and "rehearsals" at Gillespie's apartment, they practically played their instruments around the clock. In this pressure cooker, testing each other with every breath, the music began to develop very quickly.

By 1942, a musician had to be a master of his chosen instrument to stay on the bandstand at Minton's. He also had to understand musical theory so completely that he could play a song in a variety of keys, improvising the chords without hesitation. If a person played a rhythm instrument, he had to be able to move in and out of that role while experimenting as a soloist; if he played a melody or lead instrument, he had to be able to keep time in his head (for he could not rely on any single instrument to hold the beat), while the group constantly switched tempos, seemingly at whim.

This exhilarating challenge drew to Harlem the best and most daring musicians of the era. Those who could keep up found themselves with a whole new range of harmonies and rhythms to play. It was as if a painter were given a palette of colors he or she had never seen before.

The critics, however, came down hard. Many swing musicians called the new sound "chaos," and the "moldy figs" who specialized in original Dixieland-style jazz claimed it would destroy American music. At one point, Louis Armstrong even told Gillespie, "You're making all them damned notes and nobody knows what's going on. You are a musician. You know what's going on, but those people don't." Record company executives came to Minton's and listened, but none dared to take the new-style–jazz musicians into the studio.

Gillespie changed all that when he went into the studio with the Lucky Millinder Band on July 29, 1942. The band began its recording of "Little John Special" by playing a workmanlike, swing-style rhythm groove. A routine saxophone solo followed. Then, seemingly out of nowhere, came a pair of blazingly modern choruses by Gillespie. Such colorful bursts would become a trademark of his solos in the coming years; but in 1942, when he played these choruses over a plodding rhythm section, they sounded startling and new.

Gillespie opened this solo on a high note. Next, he plummeted to the lowest register possible on his trumpet, swirled around at the bottom for a moment, then lithely snaked up to a middle range, where he blasted dazzling flurries of eighth-note triplets. One can only imagine the 24-year-old trumpeter delivering his solo on "Little John Special" as a personal manifesto, as if to say that he would no longer meet the swing style on equal terms.

Later that year, Gillespie joined a new band being put together by pianist Earl "Fatha" Hines. Shadow Wilson and Billy Eckstine, Gillespie's downstairs neighbors, signed on, along with a sassy young

vocalist who had just won the Amateur Hour contest at the Apollo Theatre, Sarah Vaughan. This crew instantly modernized the Hines band, and when Charlie Parker joined them in early 1943, Vaughan recognized that "this was the beginning of bebop." The excitement on the bandstand would sometimes become unbearable when the band tore through one of Gillespie's new compositions. "We'd get to swinging so much, Dizzy would come down and grab me and start jitterbugging all over the place," Vaughan remembered. "It was swinging!"

Gillespie soon recognized how important Parker was to his own growth as a musician. "I guess Charlie Parker and I had a meeting of the minds, because

The talent-rich Earl Hines Orchestra performing in April 1943 at the Apollo Theatre in New York City. "Earl Hines's band had something a little different," Gillespie said. "He had a lotta young guys who all wanted to play in the modern style." In addition to Gillespie (far left), the band included Charlie Parker (far right), Shadow Wilson (on drums), and Sarah Vaughan (playing piano opposite Hines).

both of us inspired each other," Dizzy said. He believed he was more advanced harmonically than the saxophonist, but Parker "heard rhythm and rhythmic patterns differently, and after we started playing together, I began to play, rhythmically, more like him." This was no small concession from a musician who always prided himself on his ability to play rhythm.

On the bandstand, Gillespie and Parker seemed to read each other's mind. They traded solos and riffed together at a level of speed and versatility far beyond anyone else, working like a two-headed musical monster. According to composer and author Gunther Schuller, it was in the Hines band that their "musical conceptions were to converge, each learning from the other in a reciprocal musical union that, considering its impact, was virtually unique in jazz history."

Unfortunately, these early collaborations were never recorded. A two-year strike by the American Federation of Musicians, a powerful union that got into a dispute with the nation's record companies, made it practically impossible for anyone to record. As a result, the Hines band became one of the great unrecorded groups in jazz history.

Before the year was out, Gillespie left Hines. Billy Eckstine wanted to put together his own orchestra, and Gillespie agreed to sign on as musical director. All the modern-style players in the Hines band joined Eckstine, and the new group toured the country, determined to expose its fresh new sound.

Eckstine's band was never recorded properly, either. But those who saw it live in 1944 say that no group has ever come close to generating that level of bewildering excitement. "They'd be playing passages and Bird would run into something that'd scare everybody to death," road manager Bob Redcross recalled. "And the same thing would happen with Diz. Diz would be playing, man, and the brass section would damn near quit."

It was not just the band members who were dazzled by Parker and Gillespie's pyrotechnics. Dancers stopped cold, their feet unable to keep up with the speed of the horns, and watched dumbfounded as the two virtuosos pushed each other toward ever more complex inventions. "It was the first band that ever played that people couldn't dance to," Redcross said.

Several times in small towns, Eckstine pulled the orchestra off the stage rather than give in to the locals' demands for a danceable swing tune. He felt that if an audience could not appreciate this chal-

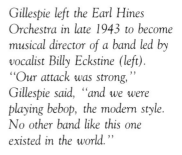

Gillespie left the Earl Hines Orchestra in late 1943 to become musical director of a band led by vocalist Billy Eckstine (left). "Our attack was strong," Gillespie said, "and we were playing bebop, the modern style. No other band like this one existed in the world."

lenging new music, they could do without it.

It was not long before a rift developed in popular music. Individual vocalists, cashing in on the growing popularity of sentimental tunes, began to step into the limelight at the expense of the big bands. Modern jazz, which was quickly evolving into a form of concert music—to be listened to attentively rather than danced to—had its own following. Caught between these two extremes, what was a dance fan to do?

Many joined a third camp, a branch of popular music that incorporated the heavy beat of blues, jump, and boogie-woogie tunes. Dubbed rhythm and blues, this camp would branch out after World War II into rock and roll, soul, disco, and funk. But in the 1940s it provided the only outlet for dancers who were left high and dry by the experiments of modern jazz.

Perhaps Gillespie could have paid more attention to the desires of this large part of his audience. Perhaps he could have found a way to shape an intellectually challenging music that still brought the dancers to their feet. Yet Gillespie recognized better than anyone else that the music he was creating could not be compromised.

Among other things, modern jazz forced its audience to salute the undeniable artistry of black composers and musicians once and for all. Divorced from the old stereotypes of "jungle music" and "happy feet," reinforced for so long by vaudeville and the swing bands, modern jazz demanded that its listeners drop their prejudices and appreciate a music unmatched in invention and intellectual rigor since the golden age of the classical composers. Its emphasis on spontaneous improvisation made it unique among all musical forms.

Thanks to his exposure as a trumpeter, composer, and musical director in Eckstine's band, Gillespie won an *Esquire* magazine New Star Award in its 1944 jazz poll. That summer, the managers of the Onyx Club on 52nd Street in midtown Manhattan asked him to put together a band along with bassist Oscar Pettiford. Dizzy accepted the offer and left Eckstine's troupe after just seven months. His new band, he said later, "put us on the map. The opening of the Onyx Club represented the birth of the bebop era."

One block along West 52nd Street soon became the hottest music spot in the world. It held a dozen jazz clubs, some of which catered entirely to Dixieland players. Other night spots featured swing musicians. And, beginning with the Onyx Club, a few began to book the modern jazz experimenters. A second generation of modernists was all set to follow in the footsteps of the pioneers: bassist Billy Taylor, drummer Max Roach, saxophonist Dexter Gordon, trumpeter Miles Davis, and pianist Bud Powell would help define the shape of jazz in the postwar years.

Along with them came a new generation of jazz lovers for whom the harsh melodies, dissonant harmonies, and breathtaking tempos of the new music carried a powerful message. To these fans, it was a liberating sound born at a time of global war, with the world on the verge of the atomic age. They did not regard the music as chaotic; they heard in it the rallying cry of a reckless, terrifying era.

Dizzy Gillespie knew that modern jazz demanded more—of performer and listener—than any music that had preceded it. He recognized that resistance to its spread would come hard and heavy. For many people, what was so special about modern jazz—that it was intellectually challenging and that it was created by black artists—made it a difficult thing to swallow. Yet he was determined to win advocates one at a time, if necessary. On 52nd Street, he set out to do exactly that. ◀◉▶

5

THE BEBOP CRUSADE

B Y THE TIME Dizzy Gillespie returned to the New York scene in the summer of 1944, West 52nd Street between Fifth and Sixth avenues had become *the* hotbed of jazz. A listener strolling along the block-long strip at night could piece together the entire history of jazz just from the music that wafted out of the doorways. Dixieland ensembles performed next door to swing bands; across the street were jump bands; down the block played modern jazz improvisers.

The best musicians in each field worked there. They kept an ear out for new sounds and sat in with each other at the various clubs. Rivalries were intense. Not since the infancy of jazz, when the Dixieland sound was born on a few blocks in downtown New Orleans, had so much musical creativity centered on such a small tract of land. As one person said of the Manhattan strip, "It was a Street of stars."

While he put together a band at the Onyx Club with Oscar Pettiford, Gillespie worked with Coleman Hawkins's band. He also filled in for four weeks with the Duke Ellington Orchestra at Broadway's Capital Theater.

"I didn't play any solos in Duke's band," Gillespie recalled, "until one guy, I don't remember who, missed the show, and somebody had to play his solo.

Gillespie at the corner of 52nd Street and Sixth Avenue in New York City. Beginning in the mid-1940s, the stretch of 52nd Street between Fifth and Sixth avenues became known to music lovers everywhere as the Street—the mecca for every form of jazz, particularly bebop.

63

And then Duke pointed to me; and he pointed to me again, again, again, and again. I kept playing. I don't know how many choruses. He just kept pointing at me, saying, 'Another one. . . .' Until I just sat down." A master bandleader, Ellington knew how to get the most out of his musicians. He handled his personnel so deftly, in fact, that his orchestra was like a musical instrument in his hands.

The band that Gillespie wound up putting together with Pettiford was much smaller than Ellington's orchestra. The first person Gillespie and Pettiford tried to hire was Charlie Parker, but he was unavailable. In his place, they enlisted a blazing young saxophonist, Don Byas, then added Max Roach and pianist George Wallington. By choosing Wallington, who was white, Gillespie became one of the first bandleaders in America to hire musicians regardless of their skin color.

Pettiford wrote songs constantly, as did Gillespie, so the Gillespie-Pettiford Quintet had an entire sheaf of original tunes. What they did not have was a name for the startling new sounds they were making.

Because it was all but impossible to notate these new songs, Gillespie would hum the passages to his bandmates to indicate how he wanted them played. According to saxophonist Budd Johnson, "He'd say, 'oop bop ta oop a la doo bop doo ba.' So people said, 'Play some more of that bebop.' And actually, that's how I think it got its name, bebop."

Jazz critics were quick to pick up on the new word. When Gillespie obliged them by titling one of his new tunes "Bebop," the music he had been tinkering with for years finally had a catchy name.

Gillespie was quick to understand that for bebop to gain an appreciable audience, he would have to continue getting the sound down on disc. He had already recorded the first bebop tunes on February 16, 1944, shortly after the recording ban ended. Joining

him in the studio for that session were Pettiford, Byas, Roach, Hawkins, Johnson, and several others. Gillespie contributed an extraordinary new song, "Woody 'n' You," that he named after bandleader Woody Herman, a vocal supporter of the music. It contained both a melody and a countermelody, and the swooping blend of the two has since made the song one of the best-loved jazz compositions of all time.

Gillespie realized that for pieces such as "Woody 'n' You" to capture the public's attention, he had to get the critics interested in bebop. Fortunately, the 52nd Street clubs were situated just around the corner from several recording studios; their midtown location made it easy for critics to keep track of what was going on in the jazz world.

Gillespie performs at the Onyx Club, on 52nd Street, with (from left to right) drummer Max Roach, saxophonist Budd Johnson, bassist Oscar Pettiford, and pianist George Wallington. "As a musician I think Dizzy has no peer," Roach said. "He's inspired perhaps more musicians who are out here today than you can shake a stick at."

Pettiford, however, was not a reliable partner when it came to popularizing bebop. He often showed up drunk, and it showed in his music. When Gillespie could take no more of Pettiford's inconsistent playing, the two of them agreed to dissolve the band. Gillespie promptly started a new group that appeared regularly at the Downbeat Club, located across the street from the Onyx. In fact, during the years that followed, he would be able to land gigs on 52nd Street whenever he wanted them.

A 1940s view of 52nd Street, looking east from Sixth Avenue. Young musicians and veterans alike flocked to the block-long strip, which was home to a dozen lively jazz clubs, bars, and restaurants.

The most significant of these gigs took place at a club called the Three Deuces. Shortly after Labor Day, 1944, the Three Deuces hired Charlie Parker, who had just left Billy Eckstine's orchestra. Within a matter of weeks, Gillespie hooked up with Bird and helped him put together a new group. Max Roach, Bud Powell, and bassist Ray Brown rounded out the ensemble that would change the sound of jazz forever.

As in Eckstine's band, Dizzy's trumpet and Bird's saxophone combined with breathtaking results.

"Yard and I were like two peas," Gillespie wrote in *To Be or Not to Bop*. "Our music was like putting whipped cream on jello. His contribution and mine just happened to go together, like putting salt in rice. . . . Sometimes I couldn't tell whether I was playing or not because the notes were so close together. He was always going in the same direction as me."

After years of appearing with musicians who needed to be encouraged to stop playing swing, Gillespie was finally working in a small group with a bandmate who instinctively understood how to play modern jazz. "Let's not call it bebop," Parker insisted. "Let's call it music." But no matter by what name the new sound was known, no two people played it better than Dizzy and Bird. According to Gillespie, "The height of the perfection of our music occurred in the Three Deuces with Charlie Parker."

Before long, all of 52nd Street knew about the wonders occurring nightly at the Three Deuces. Not everyone was convinced, however. Most recording executives remained leery about the commercial potential of bebop.

That began to change in early 1945, when Gillespie and Parker took four other musicians into the studio. Unlike today, musicians in the 1940s recorded without the benefit of being able to overdub an instrument if the take was not perfect. The band members had to get everything right. Often, the musicians arrived at the studio late at night, still warmed up from their club performance.

Gillespie and the others recorded "Groovin' High" and "Dizzy Atmosphere" in February and March. In May, the Dizzy Gillespie All-Star Quintet, featuring Parker on saxophone, recorded "Salt Peanuts." It would become one of Gillespie's best-known compositions.

When these discs were released, young musicians were able for the first time to replay Gillespie and

Parker's high-velocity improvisations, figure out what the two musicians were doing, and then try to emulate the sound. Across the country, in California, bassist Red Callender recalled, "We used to play these records—we'd get in a room and live with them all night. It was unbelievable. Something from outer space." Saxophonist Art Pepper recalled that after he listened to the records, "I said, 'Oh my God,' and I just got sick. I just couldn't believe it. I couldn't listen to any more at the moment." Trumpeter Chico O'Farrill said after he first heard the Gillespie-Parker tune "Things to Come": "If this is the shape of things to come, how in the hell am I going to cut it?"

The response was no different from the musicians who came to hear Gillespie and Parker live at the Three Deuces. By this time, Gillespie had reached awesome prowess on his trumpet. Not only could he reach higher notes than anyone else, but he could actually play complex phrases at the top of his range, instead of just reaching for single notes. No one could insert as many notes into a chord or could play as fast. He was the only trumpeter alive who could keep up with Charlie Parker's saxophone and at the same time create intricate, flexible solos. Horn men stood at the bar and cried when they heard Gillespie's work. Trumpeter Duke Garrett has gone so far as to say, "Some of us right today never have gotten down to his technique."

Meanwhile, Gillespie was having the time of his life. He and Parker would sometimes hide their instruments under their coats and sneak onto the stage at other clubs on 52nd Street. Their presence would quickly clear the stage. No one dared to challenge them.

After they had called it a night, Gillespie would occasionally hear a knock on the front door to his apartment in the wee hours of the morning. Parker, who did not know how to write down music, would be standing in the hallway, having come up with a

The Gillespie-Parker Quintet dazzles the crowd during a 1945 concert at New York City's Town Hall. "The important thing about our music," Gillespie said, "was, of course, the style, how you got from one note to another, how it was played."

new phrase that he liked and wanted Gillespie to note down. Whenever Dizzy let Bird in, the two musicians would spend the rest of the morning playing and talking about a wide range of subjects, anything from Eastern philosophy to French poetry to the latest news about the atom bomb, which was then being developed. Because of that, Lorraine sometimes refused to let the saxophonist into the apartment. When that happened, her husband would drag himself to the piano and transcribe the music while Parker stood outside, softly playing his alto saxophone.

In mid-1945, disc jockey Symphony Sid, along with publicists Monte Kay and Mal Braveman, sponsored a concert for the Gillespie-Parker Quintet at the large venue Town Hall in New York. The group was received enthusiastically, and critics began to write that the two musicians were now *the* forces to be reckoned with in jazz. These words of praise convinced Gillespie to go back on the road, but to do that, he needed a big band. "I made a major effort," he recalled, "to gather the best modern jazz talent available and to organize the band well so everybody could hear exactly how the cream of the crop sounded." In the trumpet section alone sat Miles Davis, Fats Navarro, Freddie Webster, and McKinley ("Kenny") Dorham—each of them a budding star.

Gillespie remembered how Cab Calloway had varied his productions with comedy and dance routines, so when the first Dizzy Gillespie Orchestra went on the road, it took along a popular dance team, Harold and Fayard Nicholas; a pair of 300-pound comedians, Patterson and Jackson; and a shimmy dancer, Lovey Lane, who was hired to keep the audience interested during the slower numbers. Gillespie called the production Hepsations 1945, and the tour's promoters booked it into dance halls across the southern United States, where it was hoped the region's large black population would take to the new sounds.

Unfortunately for Gillespie's first big band, audiences came to the show expecting to do more than listen and watch—jazz, after all, had its roots in dance music. Even the Nicholas Brothers found it difficult to dance to bebop. "I would listen to this bebop music," Fayard Nicholas said, "and I tried it, maybe I would create different steps to it to fit the music. And it worked out. Sure you can do it, if you just put your mind to it and get with it."

Generally, however, the audiences could not make sense of the music. Sometimes, they booed. At other times, they just walked out, leaving a stageful of the finest jazz musicians in the world playing for each other in an empty hall.

Gillespie refused to compromise his music so people could dance to it more easily. To him, the dance tunes that others were playing sounded "like pretty, manufactured meaningless tinsel rolling off an assembly line." He returned to New York disheartened by the South's poor reception of bebop but more determined than ever to push on.

Gillespie joined forces with Parker once more, only to see the specter of drug use rear its ugly head. Parker had been a heroin addict since he was a teenager, but it was only now that the drug visibly began to affect his performance. He often arrived late for shows or nodded out on the bandstand.

Gillespie, who looked forward to challenging interplay from his musical soulmate, could not stand to see Parker lose himself to drugs. To Gillespie, bebop had become a crusade. The 28-year-old trumpeter recognized that many racial, musical, and economic obstacles stood in the way of popularizing the new music. He knew it would take musicians with clear heads and an almost religious dedication to nurture bebop.

Even though Gillespie was widely known for being a practical joker and onstage comic, he had always taken his music extremely seriously. His enthusiasm had always proved infectious with the other boppers. They thrived on his encouragement, taking risks they would never have attempted on their own, thinking of themselves as a team of rebels who had given up well-paying jobs in swing bands to forge a new sound.

And now Charlie Parker, whom everyone was calling the world's greatest saxophone player, seemed willing to throw away his life for the sake of drugs. It was a horrible thing for Gillespie to witness. Dizzy tried every trick in the book to persuade his friend to kick the habit; he even went so far as to embarrass him onstage. The whole band, in fact, pleaded with Parker to get off the stuff, only to see him shake his head wearily and walk out the door. Finally, Gillespie could stand no more. In frustration, he quit the band.

News of Gillespie's departure came as a shock to the jazz fans on 52nd Street and sent Dizzy's manager, Billy Shaw, into a frenzy. Shaw tried to figure out how to reunite the two musicians. At last, he suggested that they take the quintet to California. Perhaps the West Coast would be more receptive to bebop than the South had been, and a small band would succeed where the Hepsations orchestra had failed. At the very least, the trip would take Parker away from his drug suppliers.

Gillespie reluctantly agreed, on the condition that vibraphonist Milt Jackson could come along. That way, if Parker continued to miss performances, Jackson could take the stage, and the audience would still hear a quintet. Shaw liked the sound of that. So, in late 1945, Gillespie and his wife, Lorraine; Parker; Jackson; Ray Brown; pianist Al Haig; and drummer Stan Levey boarded a fancy new Super Constellation propeller airplane for the first transcontinental flight of their life. When the musicians arrived at Billy Berg's nightclub in Los Angeles, they became the first bebop band—and, because Haig and Levey were white, the first racially integrated jazz band—ever to play on the West Coast.

For Gillespie, the first week of their engagement was "magic." Parker played with gusto, movie stars arrived in droves to hear the new sound they had read about, and jazz musicians lined up at the bar, bedazzled. Then Parker's drugs ran out. Searching

The beginning of the end: Charlie Parker in early 1946, when his drug addiction problems caused him to miss a number of performances at Billy Berg's Los Angeles nightclub. Gillespie was eventually forced to replace Parker in the band with saxophonist Lucky Thompson.

frantically for more, he disappeared for days at a time.

Gillespie was forced to replace him with another saxophonist. Then, when Parker finally did show up, he threw fits about there being too many performers onstage. According to Levey, by then "Parker was a basket case."

To make matters worse, the music was failing to take hold. By the end of the first week, most Californians seemed as puzzled by bebop as audiences had been in the South. They seemed to prefer the opening act, a guitar-comedy team, to Gillespie's compositions.

When the band's contract ran out in early February 1946, Gillespie breathed a sigh of relief. Even a snowy winter in New York would be preferable to the icy reception he had received in California. Yet when the time came to leave for the East Coast, Parker was nowhere to be found. Many bandleaders would have left the troubled reedman to fend for himself, but not Gillespie. A search was conducted for the wayward Bird. While waiting around, Dizzy went into the studio and recorded "'Round About Midnight" and a few other songs.

Parker, however, never turned up. No one in the band knew it at the time, but Parker, unable to support his drug habit on the West Coast, had suffered a nervous breakdown and lay trembling in a bed at Camarillo State Hospital.

Eventually, the band left California without Parker. As the plane droned eastward and the broad continent scrolled slowly beneath him, Gillespie looked forward to returning to 52nd Street and putting the travails of California behind him. He and Bird, the person Dizzy called "my closest friend and colleague," would play and record together a few more times. But for all practical purposes, the most dynamic duo in jazz history had gone their separate ways. ❦

6

BIG BAND BOP

EVEN THOUGH THE rest of the country still did not appreciate bebop, New York City by 1946 could not seem to get enough of it. Club owners on 52nd Street fell over each other as they competed to hire Gillespie. At last, he accepted an offer from Clark Monroe, who owned a large nightclub called the Spotlite. Monroe won Gillespie over by offering to help him rebuild his big band.

Gillespie immediately hired Thelonius Monk, Max Roach, Ray Brown, Milt Jackson, and saxophone player Sonny Stitt. They went to work performing the new songs Gillespie had been writing daily. Monk, one of the jazz world's most original composers, added his own tunes. To arrange this new music for a big band, Gillespie hired Gil Fuller. Thus began a partnership between Gillespie and Fuller that would prove productive for many years.

As always, Gillespie's ambitions were large. He sought nothing less than to translate the intimate, high-velocity interactions of a small group into the more unwieldy performance of a big band. Fuller, inspired by the challenge, seemed to instinctively understand the trumpeter's ideas.

To help promote the spread of bebop in the mid-1940s, Gillespie began to form his own jazz groups, ranging in size from quintets to big bands. He proved to be one of the first black bandleaders to hire musicians without regard to their race.

For several weeks, word that Gillespie was putting together a big band spread among jazz lovers; these fans could actually watch the ensemble grow onstage as additional members crowded onto the bandstand each night. When the full orchestra performed for the first time in February 1946, it did not let the audience down. Standing backstage, Fuller grinned at the response. "Well," he said of the opening-night crowd at the Spotlite, "they weren't expecting that noise, the whole band, a little club, and this first thing started with the whole band hitting one note. And Dizzy brought his hand up, and everybody jumped. And by the time they landed on their feet, thinking it was over—no, he hit another one—another one—another one!"

Jazz critic Leonard Feather, who sat spellbound in the audience that night, wasted no time trying to get the orchestra into a major label's recording studio. He succeeded, convincing the wary executives at RCA records to give bebop a chance. On February 22, 1946, the big band recorded three tunes, Gillespie's "52nd Street Theme," his haunting "A Night in Tunisia," and Charlie Parker's beautiful "Anthropology." On the last of these pieces, Gillespie cut loose with a stunning, high-octave chorus that no other trumpeter alive could have achieved. These songs quickly became jazz standards, and they are still performed around the world almost every night.

Parker joined the band when he returned from California, bringing along the young trumpeter Miles Davis. They would not stay long. Some of Parker's performances with Gillespie's big band recalled the high points of his days at the Three Deuces. Drugs continued to take a toll on his work, however, and after he fell asleep onstage during a show in the Bronx, Gillespie had no choice but to fire his friend. Davis left the band shortly thereafter to form a small combo with Bird.

Gillespie swoons to the sounds of the First Lady of Song, vocalist Ella Fitzgerald, who joined his big band in 1946.

Gillespie had to let Thelonius Monk go as well. As talented as the shy pianist was, he almost never arrived for work on time. Like Parker and Davis, he too formed his own group, and during the next decade he would create an enduring body of music that gradually helped change the sound of jazz.

Meanwhile, Gillespie tried out all sorts of combinations until he found bandmates who shared his single-minded dedication to bebop. Saxophonists James Moody and Joe Gayles and trumpeter Dave Burns joined the band straight out of the U.S. Army. They regarded Gillespie's orchestra as a sort of graduate school of jazz. The rhythm section—Kenny Clarke, John Lewis, Milt Jackson, and Ray Brown—developed such a camaraderie that in later years these four musicians would form their own band, the influential Modern Jazz Quartet. In 1946, though, they all thrilled to Gillespie's exuberant musical conceptions.

The 28-year-old trumpeter had not forgotten his years sitting impatiently in all those swing bands, and now that he had his own orchestra, he was determined to allow his musicians all the creative freedom they needed onstage. When the time arrived to take the band on the road, Gillespie could rest easy, knowing that he had built the orchestra in his own image, with bandmates who loved a challenge, did not take drugs, rehearsed constantly, and lived to make music.

Gillespie hired Ella Fitzgerald as his singer and made sure that this time around the band was booked into theaters and not into dance halls. Even so, there were nights when the music came so powerfully that he could not keep his feet still. "Yeah, we danced like mad together," Fitzgerald recalled. "Dizzy was a good dancer. Both of us were good dancers. And we'd go with the old Savoy steps."

Gillespie especially enjoyed performing near his schoolboy stomping grounds. The band was rehearsing in Columbia, South Carolina, one afternoon when who should turn up onstage at Township Auditorium but Dizzy's grade school music teacher, Alice Wilson. Overjoyed, he grabbed her and spun her around, then introduced her to the band. "She's the one that taught me all the jazz I know, man," he told his fellow musicians. "She started me off with it."

Gillespie's meeting with Alice Wilson was not the only reunion that took place in the South. When the big band played in Maxton, North Carolina, near his hometown of Cheraw, his relatives and friends crowded into the audience. He even returned to the Laurinburg Technical Institute and performed there with his troupe. The experience, he said, "made me feel very proud and reminded me of how very narrowly I'd missed spending my days behind a mule."

The tour proved to be a great success, wiping away the bad memories from Gillespie's previous expedition through the South in 1945. His band was so popular, in fact, that a concert movie, called *Jivin' in Bebop*, was made following the tour. A youthful Gillespie appeared in the film skipping about the stage, pausing only to cue the band or bring the trumpet to his lips for an extended solo. By this time, the 15-member band showed itself to be so accomplished it could shift gears at a snap of the bandleader's fingers. Whenever he played his horn, the eyes of the other trumpeters looked on with unfeigned admiration.

Gillespie had tap dancers, belly dancers, Lindy Hoppers, and even dancers in African garb leaping about the stage during various songs, as if determined to prove that bebop *could* be danced to. The feet of one talented dancer became a blur as he tapped out the rhythm to a high-velocity "Ornithology."

To top it all off, Gillespie proved himself a surprisingly smooth-voiced vocalist by singing a novelty tune, "He Beeped When He Should Have Bopped." The song made fun of all those musicians who could not keep up with the technical demands of modern jazz.

After the orchestra returned to New York, it performed at prestigious Carnegie Hall on September 29, 1947. That show prompted many critics to write that bebop had replaced swing as the leading style of jazz. William Gottlieb wrote in the *New York Herald Tribune*, "The music in spite of its name is not nonsense." Bebop is more modern, more progressive, and better suited to the times than other jazz forms, he said.

As pleased as Gillespie was by these comments, he was touched even more deeply by a personal tribute. During the show, Charlie Parker appeared onstage just long enough to present the bandleader

An advertisement for Jivin' in Bebop, *the 1947 concert film that featured Gillespie and his big band.*

with a single red rose. Parker, who was continuing his long slide downward, "probably spent his last quarter to buy it," Gillespie later said. Bird gave Dizzy a kiss on the lips and then vanished.

Following the big band's appearance at Carnegie Hall, the awards started to roll in for Gillespie. The jazz magazine *Metronome* named him Trumpet of the Year in 1947, as it would for the next three years, and his orchestra Band of the Year. Swing bandleaders, including Benny Carter and Stan Kenton, scrambled to update their own music to keep pace with Gillespie's orchestra. But his ideas were evolving so quickly that other groups were left hopelessly behind.

For instance, Gillespie had just recorded three new songs that introduced an unusual new element: a conga drummer. Gillespie had been interested in the sophisticated rhythms played by drummers from the Caribbean ever since moonlighting in Latin bands during the 1930s. By introducing these poly-rhythms to jazz, Gillespie also meant to retrieve a part of his racial heritage: the sounds of African tribal drumming, a traditional form of communication that enslaved blacks were unable to practice in America centuries earlier, when slaveholders confiscated their slaves' drums to prevent them from "talking" to one another.

Gillespie did not make conga drums a regular part of his band's rhythm section until he met Cuban drummer Luciano Pozo y Gonzales, who was also known as Chano Pozo. Mario Bauza introduced the two men. Even though Gillespie could not speak Spanish and Pozo spoke only broken English, they understood each other perfectly. Both found common ground in their love of African-based rhythms.

In fact, Pozo soon had every member of the band involved in performing sophisticated cross-rhythms. When the orchestra was touring, he would teach them by beating his hands on the seats of the bus. For

Gillespie had good reason to strut across the Carnegie Hall stage in 1947: The concert given by his big band broke attendance records at the prestigious New York City music hall.

the most part, though, he worked closely with Dizzy. They co-wrote the masterpiece "Manteca" and rearranged a two-part tune that Gillespie co-wrote, "Cubana Be, Cubana Bop." Whenever the orchestra performed the latter song, Pozo would lead an authentic African chant, with the band members answering in unison.

Dizzy Gillespie's Big Band recorded these songs in December 1947, then began to perform them on tour. The audience responded wildly to this radical new musical hybrid. Gillespie recalled, "It was similar to a nuclear weapon, when it burst on the scene, the merger of Cuban and American music, they had never seen before."

Gillespie had already done much to modernize jazz music, and now he forged the first definitive breakthrough from the old swing beat. Duke Elling-

ton had experimented with polyrhythmic compositions, and most swing bands included Latin-style
novelty tunes in their performances. But no bandleader had ever hired a Cuban conga drummer to
change the sound of his orchestra. The effect of
Gillespie's collaboration with Chano Pozo is still
being felt today as jazz and other forms of popular
music continue to absorb the musical traditions of
other cultures in the creation of exciting new sounds.

During the first three months of 1948, Dizzy
Gillespie's Big Band toured Europe, where they were
greeted with wild applause at every stop. The orchestra responded with one remarkable performance after
another. Pozo, having oiled his body beforehand,
would appear onstage without a shirt, chanting to the
band while pounding a conga drum that was strapped
to his back. Gillespie was amazed at how Pozo could
dance to one rhythm, sing another, and play an
entirely different beat on his drums. The crowds sat
there, awestruck.

Kenny Clarke was so impressed by the respect
European audiences showed the band that he decided
to stay in Paris after the tour. Offered a position at a
university to teach drumming techniques, he bid his
old friend Gillespie good-bye. The two had once
stood alone in advocating their new musical ideas.
Now a whole generation of jazz musicians was carrying on their work.

Gillespie returned to the United States more
popular than ever. All over the country, crowds
stood on line for hours to hear his band. In California, he even won over West Coast audiences with a
dazzling eight-week tour. Two years earlier, he and
Charlie Parker had played to just a few fans in Los
Angeles; now the crowds there could hardly fit in the
door.

Everywhere he went, bebop fans wore a beret,
Gillespie's trademark hat. Teenage girls even painted

By featuring the Cuban percussionist Chano Pozo (center) in the orchestra in 1947, Gillespie became the first person to introduce Afro-Cuban rhythms into modern jazz. Saxophonist James Moody, who played with Gillespie for almost eight years, is at left.

a copy of his goatee on their chin. Disc jockeys such as Chicago's Daddy-O Daylie spread the inside language of bebop far and wide, until Gillespie had to chuckle when he heard kids using words such as *hip*, *square*, and *jive*. His music had certainly struck a chord with young people. They loved its speed, its rebellious energy, the way it seemed to break all the rules. Perhaps they could not appreciate the sophisticated harmonies and rhythms, but what they could understand, they swore by.

The one thing about Gillespie that none of the youngsters could copy was the way his cheeks had begun to puff out when he put the trumpet to his lips. To this day, Gillespie cannot explain exactly why it began to happen. "I didn't get any physical pain from it," he said of this phenomenon, "but all of a sudden,

Gillespie confers with (from right to left) saxophonist John Brown, pianist John Lewis, and saxophonist Joe Gayles. At this 1947 recording session, Dizzy Gillespie and His Orchestra cut four tunes, including "Oop-Pop-A-Da," which became Gillespie's first bebop vocal hit.

I looked like a frog whenever I played." With his characteristic sense of humor, Gillespie laughed the whole thing off and kept right on performing his unbeatable solos.

Following his successful return to California, Gillespie and his band toured the South with Ella Fitzgerald. Along the way, the orchestra stopped off once more at the Laurinburg Technical Institute, and this time the high school's principal was ready for the bandleader's arrival. In a special ceremony before the concert, Gillespie was awarded his varsity football letter and was handed his high school diploma. Thirteen years earlier, he had left his schoolbooks behind in North Carolina. But from this day on, a proud Gillespie admitted, he would no longer have to think of himself as a dropout.

Pozo dropped out of the tour the following week, when his congas were stolen from the orchestra's bus. A few days later, word reached the band that Pozo had been shot in a Harlem bar, in a dispute over money. According to the bartender, Pozo had just put "Manteca" on the jukebox when the gun went off. He died before the song had finished playing.

The Dizzy Gillespie Big Band closed an otherwise successful 1948 on Christmas night, when it again played at Carnegie Hall. Charlie Parker joined the orchestra for a few tunes, along with Miles Davis and other members of the bebop fraternity. Jazz critics dubbed the event a "bop summit conference."

A few weeks later, Leonard Feather published his book *Inside Bebop*. It was the first scholarly look at modern jazz—and yet another sign that the old swing establishment had crumbled. In just one decade, Gillespie had seen his dream come true: The expressive possibilities available to a jazz artist now seemed all but unlimited. As an unparalleled performer, visionary composer, patient teacher, and indefatigable bandleader, Gillespie himself was largely responsible for spreading the new music across the United States and Europe. Dizzy Gillespie now set his sights on the rest of the world. ❧

7

WORLDWIDE JAZZ AMBASSADOR

Dizzy Gillespie Believes his big band of the late 1940s was the best orchestra he ever led. Most of the members had been with him for several years. They had absorbed the Afro-Cuban rhythmic influences he favored, and on the bandstand they came as close as any 15-piece unit ever would to the intimate interactions of a small group.

Yet it is clear from their recorded output that by 1950 the Dizzy Gillespie Big Band was struggling to survive. Audiences' tastes had continued to evolve, and they now seemed to want one of two things: singers or dance tunes. Gillespie's sophisticated concert jazz never really fit either bill.

For his records, he brought in the best of the bebop vocalists, including Johnny Hartman and Joe Carroll, and he sang novelty tunes such as "Jump Did-le Ba" himself. In every case, the orchestral performances outclassed the lyrics; it was clear that adding a singer only cheapened the band's music. When it came to creating dance tunes, Gillespie would not compromise. He had always been able to find the dance steps to fit his band's rhythms, and he was disappointed that the public could not keep up.

Out of frustration one night before a show, Dizzy asked his wife, Lorraine, a former first-line dancer at the Cotton Club, to mingle with the audience and

Gillespie in traditional Nigerian dress. According to family lore, his great-great-grandfather was chief of an African tribe.

see what the people thought. She came backstage afterward and delivered the withering verdict: "A dance band you are not!"

Gillespie's orchestra was not the only big band in trouble. Ever since World War II ended in 1945, swing bands had been folding. Gillespie and his bebop cohorts, of course, had a lot to do with this decline, for their modern music had instantly outdated the swing orchestras. But the clamor for singers and rhythm-and-blues dance bands had an even larger impact. Even though he was fronting the most adventurous orchestra in the United States, Gillespie found it tougher and tougher to find bookings. At last, in 1950, he closed out an engagement at the Silhouette Club in Chicago and broke up the band.

Back in New York, Charlie Parker and Thelonius Monk had kept busy in small groups, and Miles Davis had formed his own quintet. Davis toned down the harsher elements of bebop to create a spacious bluesy sound. His cool jazz quickly found an admiring public. Meanwhile, Max Roach and Art Blakey had gone in the other direction, pushing the tough rhythms and earthy tones of bebop. They called their music hard bop.

The rhythm section from Gillespie's orchestra proceeded to carve out a middle ground. They formed the Modern Jazz Quartet, whose tasteful arrangements and scintillating performances would find an enormous audience in the years ahead.

Having worked with all of these musicians during the formative years of bebop, Gillespie could only marvel at the way the music continued to evolve. For the first time in his career, he had to scramble to keep up with all the new variations. He traveled light for a while, fronting rhythm sections at clubs in New York, joining the all-star Jazz at the Philharmonic troupe, and recording in a wide range of settings.

In 1951, Gillespie took the bold step of founding his own record company, which he named with his

Trumpeter Miles Davis on the bandstand with Gillespie in the late 1950s. Gillespie began to play a horn with an upturned bell in 1953, after he discovered that an odd-shaped trumpet delivered its sound to his ears more quickly than a standard trumpet did. It also enabled him to keep from blasting his music into another performer's ears on a small bandstand.

initials. He later said of his decision to form Dee Gee Records that of all the boppers, "I was probably the only one around with the desire, the resources and the guts to try it." Now he would be able to produce his own recordings. Just as important, he could keep much more of the money that his records earned than he could when he worked for someone else's company. A music-loving truck driver he knew, Dave Usher, joined him in the business, and Gillespie set to work.

On March 1, the trumpeter recorded two new songs that would become signature pieces, "Birk's Works" and "Tin Tin Deo." But fearing that listeners might shy away from straight-ahead bebop, Gillespie was soon recording dance songs, calypsos, spirituals, and blues. When he did that, other boppers criticized him for going commercial instead of sticking with the form he had helped create.

To make matters worse, Usher had a difficult time keeping track of the company's finances, and Dee Gee Records immediately fell behind in paying its taxes. The Internal Revenue Service (IRS) shut down the company for good two years later. To help cover the amount of money Dee Gee Records owed,

One of the most celebrated concerts in jazz history took place in May 1953, when Gillespie held a reunion at Toronto's Massey Hall with Max Roach (left) and Charlie Parker (right), as well as pianist Bud Powell and bassist Charles Mingus.

the IRS took the company's master tapes of Gillespie's songs.

The year 1953 was by no means a complete washout for Gillespie. During a birthday party for Lorraine on January 6, someone sat on Gillespie's trumpet and bent the bell of the horn almost in half. Jokingly, Dizzy raised the battered instrument to his lips and tried to play it. The notes came out thin and breathy, yet the upturned bell got the sound to his ears more quickly than a standard trumpet did. Gillespie's eyes lit up. He went out the next day in search of a trumpet maker who could build an upturned horn. Gillespie has used such a trumpet ever since.

In May 1953, Gillespie took his new trumpet to Toronto, Canada, for a reunion concert of the band he had helped put together at the Three Deuces eight years earlier. Charlie Parker, Max Roach, Bud Powell, and Oscar Pettiford signed on for the show at cavernous Massey Hall, but the bassist had to drop out when he broke his arm playing baseball. A young Californian named Charles Mingus took Pettiford's place. As it turned out, Mingus's presence was a stroke of luck for music lovers. He sneaked a tape recorder onstage and captured an evening of remarkable music that is now available on record as *The Greatest Jazz Concert Ever* and on compact disc as *The Quintet: Jazz at Massey Hall.*

Parker arrived in Toronto without his saxophone and had to borrow a white plastic alto from a local music store. On "Perdido," the first song on the album, a listener can hear him getting used to the horn's sound. But by the time the band charges into the high-spirited "Salt Peanuts" and the breathtaking improvisations of "Wee," he is clearly at the top of his form. He and Gillespie trade solos as in the old days, with such empathy that it is difficult to tell which of them is playing during some high-velocity passages. The band closed out the evening with Gillespie's exotic "A Night in Tunisia," which more than any other song has become *the* anthem of bebop.

The following year, 1954, Gillespie performed in Newport, Rhode Island, at the first ever Newport Jazz Festival. Promoter George Wein was determined to make the show, which was the first major jazz festival ever held in the United States, a serious affair. At first, he asked Gillespie not to clown around onstage; but he soon realized his mistake and apologized, saying, "Here [is] an artist with a comic timing ability that rivals that of the geniuses like Charlie Chaplin . . . and here I am, a young punk telling him not to clown!"

Irrepressible as always, Gillespie laughed the warning off. Whenever he began to joke around onstage, he would turn toward Wein and say, "Boo!"

In early 1955, Gillespie was leading a quintet at Birdland, a bebop club near 52nd Street that was named in honor of Charlie Parker. Parker, meanwhile, was leading his own group at an uptown club. His behavior had become so erratic in recent years, however, that he was not even allowed to perform at the club that was named after him.

In the first week of March, during a show at Birdland, Gillespie spotted Parker waving to him from the audience and went over to speak with the saxophonist between sets. But Parker looked so overweight and was so shabbily dressed that Gillespie did not know what to say.

Suddenly, Parker clutched Gillespie's hand and uttered two desperate words: "Save me."

A stunned Gillespie asked, "What could I do?"

"I don't know," Parker replied, "but just save me, save me, man."

Gillespie stood there, dumbfounded. He could not forget all those times when he had pleaded with Parker to give up drugs. What more, indeed, could he do for his friend?

A week later, Lorraine Gillespie arrived at her Long Island home and heard sobbing sounds coming from the basement. She went down the steps and found her husband crying like a baby.

"What is it, Diz?" she asked.

"Charlie Parker is dead."

Parker was only 34 years old when he had his fatal heart attack on March 12. He had abused his body so terribly, however, that the medical examiner, not knowing Parker's actual age, listed it as 53.

As soon as Gillespie pulled himself together, he organized a benefit concert to help pay for Parker's funeral expenses and made sure the body was flown

home to Kansas City for burial. One of the most important figures in American music, Charlie Parker had died without a penny to his name.

Sadly, Parker did not live to see the remarkable changes his music wrought. Later in 1955, the Lenox School of Jazz in Massachusetts established a program to teach students about the complex changes of bebop. Gillespie was subsequently hired as a faculty member. In 1956, the U.S. State Department officially recognized the importance of modern jazz by asking him to tour the world as a goodwill ambassador.

Gillespie leaped at the chance to take his music on a worldwide tour. The State Department provided enough money to rebuild his orchestra and made all

There has never been a relationship that had a greater effect on the jazz world than the one between Gillespie and Charlie Parker. Gillespie still maintained nearly 25 years after his friend's death in 1955, "I get a warm feeling every time I think of Charlie Parker."

Gillespie playing the role of goodwill ambassador at a 1956 concert in South America. He was the first orchestra leader ever invited by the U.S. State Department to form a band to tour overseas.

the travel arrangements, too. If Gillespie was going to officially represent the United States overseas, he was determined to include a cross-section of the country's ethnic makeup in his band. For this tour, he hired what he called "a complete 'American assortment' of blacks, whites, males, females, Jews, and Gentiles." He asked trumpeter Quincy Jones to rehearse the orchestra while he fulfilled another tour commitment in Europe. Gillespie hooked up with the band when it arrived in Rome.

Gillespie made the most of his role as goodwill ambassador. Appearing in the newspapers nearly every day were photographs of the smiling bandleader riding a camel, wearing the Greek national costume, smoking a big pipe, or blowing his trumpet to charm a cobra. But when the time came to play music, he was all business. The trumpet section in his band had decided to try to outblow him every night, and as one of its members, Carl Warwick, remembered, "That was all he needed, for somebody else to egg him on." Gillespie played like a man possessed.

The audiences responded wildly. In Athens, Greece, the crowd threw off their clothes and tossed them at the ceiling. In Dacca, Pakistan, where few people had ever heard of jazz, the concertgoers did not know what to expect. They quickly caught the beat, however, and clapped along. And in Ankara, Turkey, the bandleader refused to play at a garden party for diplomats until the street urchins outside the walls were allowed inside. "I came here to play for *all* the people!" Gillespie told them. In fact, he made a point at every stop of showing that people of all races and faiths had joined together to make joyful music in his band.

Gillespie's troupe returned from this triumphant tour in high spirits. It recorded several songs during a 90-minute session for Verve Records, then took off for South America. Shortly after the band returned, it gave a magnificent performance at the third Newport Jazz Festival. This time, nobody dared to warn Gillespie not to clown around.

The members of the Dizzy Gillespie Orchestra wanted to continue touring, but as soon as the government stopped picking up the tab, there were not enough paying engagements in the United States to keep the band together. Before long, wages for the performers fell to just $30 a week. At that point, Gillespie realized he would have to throw in the towel. The third Dizzy Gillespie Orchestra disbanded on New Year's Eve, 1958, with everyone realizing that the age of the big band was over.

As always, Gillespie took advantage of the opportunities that came his way. During his world tour, he had sought out the best local musicians and had absorbed all he could of their exotic musical traditions. Using these lessons, he reshaped his own compositions, incorporating everything from Indian raga scales to Brazilian samba rhythms.

Once again, Dizzy Gillespie was leading the way. Decades before there was even a word for it, he had begun to explore new avenues into the important movement of the 1990s that is now called world music. ❧

Gillespie in Pakistan during his 1956 goodwill tour.

8

OL' MAN REBOP

DURING AN INTERVIEW in 1960, Dizzy Gillespie reflected on his remarkable career, saying, "What I want to do now is extend what I've done. When an architect builds a building, you know, and decides he wants to put on some new wings, it's still the same building. He keeps on until he's finished, and when he dies somebody else can carry on with it."

That, in large part, has been the trumpeter's approach to his work ever since. He has staked out new ground as both a performer and a composer while working in large orchestras and small group settings. At the Newport and Monterey jazz festivals, he has introduced a number of original pieces. Standouts among these more recent compositions were three long suites: the semiclassical "Perceptions"; a tone poem, "Kush," based on African musical themes; and his 40-minute tour de force, "Gillespiana."

Gillespie has taught jazz theory and composition at several major universities, including the Institute of Jazz Studies at Rutgers University. He has done much to promote music classes in the early grades in New York City and other parts of the country. Like many early beboppers, Gillespie has turned his bands into "graduate schools" by hiring young talent and tutoring these musicians on the finer points of jazz.

Over the years, Gillespie has worked harder than anyone to promote the artistry of bebop. "The first thing as far as the jazz artist is concerned," he said, "is to complete raising the respect of the jazz musician to the level of a classical musician or concert artist."

The virtuoso trumpeters Jon Faddis and Arturo San-
doval are perhaps his most famous recent disciples.

Meanwhile, Gillespie has used his celebrity in
other ways. In 1964, he even ran for president of the
United States. The campaign began when music
journalist Ralph Gleason wrote an article saying
Gillespie would make a better leader than anyone
else who was likely to run for office. After that,
reporters began to ask the trumpeter what he would
do in the White House. First, Gillespie said, he
would change the name of the president's home to
the Blues House. Next, he would make Duke Ellington secretary of state, Miles Davis head of the
Central Intelligence Agency, and the militant black
leader Malcolm X attorney general.

When another reporter asked Gillespie why he
was running for president, he replied, "Because we
need one." With that quote serving as his campaign
slogan, Dizzy suddenly found himself running a write-
in campaign against President Lyndon Johnson and
Republican senator Barry Goldwater. Unlike either
politician, Gillespie called for pulling U.S. troops
out of Vietnam and for free hospitalization and
housing for all who needed it. Sales from his campaign buttons went to the Congress of Racial Equality
(CORE) and the Southern Christian Leadership
Conference (SCLC), both of which promoted civil
rights. When Johnson won the election, Gillespie
could at least say that his write-in campaign had
helped draw attention to that issue.

In fact, Gillespie worked for the civil rights
movement throughout the 1960s, signing petitions,
joining in protest marches, and speaking out at every
opportunity for equality of the races. He also contributed money to the SCLC, which had been
founded by the Reverend Martin Luther King, Jr.,
and to other important civil rights organizations.

When touring across the country, Gillespie often
ran head-on into racial problems. Because his bands

were racially mixed, bigoted whites and blacks threatened and abused him. The prejudice he encountered
at concert halls, hotels, and restaurants left him
scrambling to keep his bandmates out of danger.

The 50-year-old jazz master was in Laurinburg,
attending Dizzy Gillespie Day on April 4, 1968,
when he heard the news that King had been killed by
an assassin's bullet. Reeling from the tragedy, Gillespie found comfort in the Baha'i faith, which

*Gillespie during his unsuccessful
bid for the 1964 presidency of the
United States. "I don't think
there was any choice," he said
after the election. "I was the only
choice for a thinking man."*

emphasizes the spiritual unity of humankind and recognizes the spiritual value of music. He has since credited this religious movement with helping him find inner peace. It may also have given him a new reason to carry on at a time when there was little left in the musical world that he had not already accomplished.

During the 1960s, explosive changes in the music world mirrored those in American society. Rock and roll, an offshoot of rhythm and blues, smothered jazz on the radio and in record sales, then branched off into rock, soul, and funk. Gillespie, like most other jazz artists, found ways to incorporate elements of these sounds into his music. But for the most part, these popular new music forms were too repetitive and unchallenging for his tastes.

In the jazz community, hard bop and cool jazz evolved into free jazz and jazz-rock fusion. Yet it has become clear that the most challenging and difficult work is still being done in the bebop idiom that Gillespie pioneered. The trumpeter himself has rarely found cause to stray far from the harmonic and rhythmic possibilities of bebop. Today, a generation of musicians who were not even born when Gillespie and Charlie Parker worked together at the Three Deuces is struggling to master the musical vocabulary these two musicians invented.

Gillespie's early recordings still sound remarkably fresh. To hear "Cubana Bop" or the Parker collaboration "Shaw Nuff" is to listen to a controlled explosion. Gillespie himself called the song "Manteca" a "nuclear bomb." These records capture the exciting demolition of an entire musical form—swing—and the creation of a freer, more agile style in its place. Gillespie and the other beboppers were the dynamite that split the world of music into many pieces.

Through it all, Gillespie has refused to slow down. In 1968, he briefly reformed his orchestra,

taking the Dizzy Reunion Big Band on a tour of Europe. Three years later, he hired former bandmates Sonny Stitt, Al McKibbon, Art Blakey, Kai Winding, and Thelonius Monk for a yearlong Giants of Jazz world tour.

Gillespie's schedule in 1989 would still have taxed a much younger man. The 72-year-old maestro played 300 performances in 27 countries, some of those with his new big band, aptly named the United Nations Orchestra. The band included many of the best musicians from several Latin American countries as well as the Gillespie stalwarts saxophonist James Moody and trombonist Slide Hampton.

In his later years, Gillespie has kept busy in the studio, too, sometimes releasing a new album every few months. In 1989, for example, he recorded a trio of very different performances. One was with the Rochester Symphony Orchestra, in which his compositions adapted well to the classical players' talents; his own playing is soulful and dynamic, especially on "Lorraine," the long piece named after his wife, with whom he would soon celebrate their 50th wedding

Gillespie performs for President Jimmy Carter at the White House in 1978. "It was below my station to aspire to the presidency of the United States," the trumpeter joked later. "My aspirations go higher than that. Running for President of a world government would be more in keeping with my interests."

Gillespie meets with Nelson Mandela in 1990, shortly after the leader of South Africa's black nationalist movement was released from prison. Mandela had been incarcerated since 1962 because of his opposition to racial segregation and white minority rule in South Africa.

anniversary. Another album captured a Latin-tinged live show with the United Nations Orchestra; on it, Gillespie clearly revels in the Latin polyrhythms he has championed for so long. The third album was an intimate duet with Max Roach; recorded in a Paris studio, Gillespie adopts a quieter, more meditative stance with his longtime friend, whispering each swift note as though it were a treasured memory.

Somehow Gillespie also found the time during 1989 to take on a starring dramatic role in a European-made film, *The Winter in Lisbon*. Along with playing a disgruntled jazzman, he composed the film's score. He was still in Europe that November when the Berlin Wall fell. As revelers began to knock down the barrier that had separated East and West Germany since 1961, he went to the wall, climbed on top, and tossed chunks of concrete to a cheering crowd.

During the last two decades, Gillespie has also had his hands full accepting all the accolades and honors showered on him. In recognition of his work in teaching jazz to the city's schoolchildren, New York presented its Handel Medallion to him in 1972. Not to be outdone, 14 different universities have bestowed honorary doctoral degrees on him.

The governments of many countries have honored him as well. Feted around the world, he has been the guest of several African nations, including Kenya and Namibia. He has also dined at the White House on several occasions. In fact, when President Jimmy Carter invited him to a White House picnic in 1978, Dizzy talked the former peanut farmer into singing the classic Gillespie composition "Salt Peanuts."

The following year, 1979, Gillespie published his long-awaited autobiography, *To Be or Not to Bop*. He and writer Al Fraser had spent five years combing through a lifetime of albums, articles, and letters, and they also interviewed many of Dizzy's acquaintances to produce this memoir. It offers a colorful portrait of a man who has never doubted the importance of his mission.

Thanks to his constant dedication, Gillespie's treasure chest now includes a Lifetime Achievement Grammy Award, the Paul Robeson Award from the Institute of Jazz Studies, and the recording industry's Duke Ellington Award. He has been honored by the Kennedy Center in Washington, D.C., for his lifetime of achievement in the performing arts, and his hometown has named a circular avenue Dizzy Gillespie Street. In an impressive ceremony in 1989, France made him a Chevalier of the Legion of Honor. President George Bush has subsequently presented Gillespie with the highest prize that can be awarded to an American artist, the National Medal of the Arts.

In spite of all this adulation, Gillespie remains a friendly, helpful, patient man, as comfortable with a beggar on the streets of New Delhi as with the president of the United States. From an impoverished home in the rural flatlands of South Carolina, he rocketed to the attention of musicians everywhere, turned the jazz world on its ear, and made the whole trip look like fun. For anyone interested in knowing more, Dizzy Gillespie adds a simple footnote: "To know me, study me very closely; give me your attention and above all come to my concert." ⬧

APPENDIX: SELECTED DISCOGRAPHY

Dizzy Gillespie's innovative music has been captured on many recordings during his seven decades on the jazz scene. The following albums highlight important phases of his development and offer a good introduction to his work.

The Development of an American Artist (Smithsonian). This album covers Gillespie's swing years and early bebop experiments. (It is available by mail order only from Smithsonian Recordings, P.O. Box 10230, Des Moines, IA 50336).

The King of Bop (Archive of Folk). Gillespie's 1940s recordings with Charlie Parker and Miles Davis in small group settings.

Dizziest (RCA). Gillespie's big-band recordings from 1946 to 1949, including his work with Chano Pozo.

Dee Gee Days (Savoy). Gillespie's output for his own record company, ranging from bebop to spirituals, from 1951 to 1953.

The Greatest Jazz Concert Ever (Prestige). The legendary bebop reunion of 1953, at Toronto's Massey Hall. (It has also been released on compact disc as *The Quintet: Jazz at Massey Hall.*)

Dizzy Gillespie with Sonny Rollins and Sonny Stitt: Duets (Verve). Gillespie's compositions for trumpet and saxophone, recorded in 1958.

An Electrifying Evening with the Dizzy Gillespie Quintet (Verve). A post–big-band concert at New York City's Museum of Modern Art, recorded in 1961.

Dizzy Gillespie Jam: Montreux '77 (Pablo). Gillespie jamming with Ray Brown, Jon Faddis, Milt Jackson, and others.

The Symphony Sessions (ProJazz). Gillespie's 1989 recording with the Rochester Symphony Orchestra.

Max + Dizzy: Paris 1989 (A & M). Gillespie's 1989 duets with Max Roach.

CHRONOLOGY

1917   Born John Birks Gillespie on October 21, in Cheraw, South Carolina

1922   Enters Robert Smalls Public School

1929   Begins to play the trombone and trumpet

1933   Graduates from public school; enters Laurinburg Technical Institute

1935   Moves to Philadelphia; joins the Frankie Fairfax Band; acquires the nickname Dizzy

1937   Moves to New York; joins the Teddy Hill Orchestra; meets Lorraine Willis

1939   Meets Kenny Clarke; joins the Cab Calloway Orchestra

1940   Composes "Pickin' the Cabbage"; meets Charlie Parker; marries Lorraine Willis

1941   Plays trumpet on first recordings of modern jazz jam sessions at Minton's Playhouse in Harlem

1942   Composes "A Night in Tunisia" and "Salt Peanuts"; forms his first quartet

1943   Makes first recordings with Charlie Parker; becomes musical director of the Billy Eckstine Orchestra

1945   Forms first Dizzy Gillespie Orchestra

1947   Meets Chano Pozo

1950   Joins Jazz at the Philharmonic tour

1951   Establishes Dee Gee Records

1953   Dee Gee Records closes; Gillespie accidentally bends bell of trumpet; appears at Massey Hall concert in Toronto

1954   Performs at first ever Newport Jazz Festival

1956   Tours the world as U.S. goodwill ambassador

1964   Runs for president of the United States

1968   Accepts the Baha'i faith

1972   Receives Handel Medallion from New York City

1979   Publishes memoir, *To Be or Not to Bop.*

1989   Named a Chevalier of the Legion of Honor by the French government

1990   Honored at the Kennedy Center in Washington, D.C.; awarded the National Medal of the Arts

FURTHER READING

Berger, Melvin. *The Trumpet Book*. New York: Lothrop, Lee & Shepard, 1978.

Chilton, John. *Jazz*. New York: MacKay, 1979.

Collier, James Lincoln. *The Making of Jazz: A Comprehensive History*. New York: Houghton Mifflin, 1978.

Davis, Miles, with Quincy Troupe. *Miles: The Autobiography*. New York: Simon & Schuster, 1989.

Feather, Leonard. *Inside Jazz*. New York: Robbins, 1949.

Frankl, Ron. *Duke Ellington*. New York: Chelsea House, 1988.

Giddins, Gary. *Celebrating Bird: The Triumph of Charlie Parker*. New York: Beech Tree Books, 1987.

———. *Riding on a Blue Note: Jazz and American Pop*. New York: Oxford University Press, 1981.

Gillespie, Dizzy, with Al Fraser. *To Be or Not to Bop*. New York: Doubleday, 1979.

Gitler, Ira. *Swing to Bop*. New York: Oxford University Press, 1985.

Horricks, Raymond. *Dizzy Gillespie*. New York: Hippocrene Books, 1984.

Kliment, Bud. *Ella Fitzgerald*. New York: Chelsea House, 1988.

Shaw, Arnold. *The Street That Never Slept*. New York: Coward, McCann & Geoghegan, 1971.

Stearns, Marshall W. *The Story of Jazz*. New York: Oxford University Press, 1956.

Tanenhaus, Sam. *Louis Armstrong*. New York: Chelsea House, 1989.

INDEX

PICTURE CREDITS

Photo by Danny Barker/Frank Driggs Collection: pp. 10, 38; The Bettmann Archive: p. 95; Photo by Dunc Butler/Frank Driggs Collection: pp. 18–19; Courtesy Cheraw Visitors Bureau: p. 31; Courtesy *down beat* Archives: pp. 83, 101; Frank Driggs Collection: pp. 74, 81, 86; Photo by Charles Fishman/Charismic Productions: p. 103; Courtesy Dizzy Gillespie and Charismic Productions: pp. 26, 29, 35, 47, 59, 96, 97, 104; Irvin Glaser/*down beat* Archives: p. 24; © William P. Gottlieb: pp. 2–3, 48, 50–51, 62, 66–67, 76–77, 79; Photo by Charles B. Nadell/Frank Driggs Collection: p. 70; Reuters/Bettmann Archive: p. 98; Schiedt: pp. 3, 13, 16, 42–43, 44, 54, 56–57, 65, 85, 91, 92; Photo by Chuck Stewart: p. 88; Photo by Keith Stowell/Frank Driggs Collection: p. 21; Courtesy Alice Wilson: p. 32

Thanks to Kim Johnson and Bill Brockschmidt of Kennedy Center Honors

TONY GENTRY holds an honors degree in history and literature from Harvard College. Formerly an award-winning news and cultural editor at WWL Newsradio in New Orleans, he now works in New York City. His poetry and short stories have been published in *The Quarterly, Turnstile,* and *Downtown.* He is also the author of *Paul Laurence Dunbar* and *Jesse Owens* in Chelsea House's BLACK AMERICANS OF ACHIEVEMENT series.

NATHAN IRVIN HUGGINS is W.E.B. Du Bois Professor of History and Director of the W.E.B. Du Bois Institute for Afro-American Research at Harvard University. He previously taught at Columbia University. Professor Huggins is the author of numerous books, including *Black Odyssey: The Afro-American Ordeal in Slavery, The Harlem Renaissance,* and *Slave and Citizen: The Life of Frederick Douglass.*